LONDON AFTER DARK

An intimate record of night life in London, and a selection of crime stories from the case book of

EX-SUPERINTENDENT
ROBERT FABIAN

LONDON

AFTER

DARK

BRITISH BOOK CENTRE
New York

CONTENTS

Part Four: *Tales of Darkness*

LIST OF ILLUSTRATIONS

IN MY FIRST BOOK, FABIAN OF THE YARD, I presented a selection of some of the many cases on which I was engaged during my service at Scotland Yard. They covered every kind of crime—murder, blackmail, theft, in fact, the whole gamut of misdoings associated with the big and little crooks of the criminal underworld. Most people when they retire leave their jobs behind them, but I now find myself as much concerned with the underworld as during the time when I was actually "on the beat." My present job involves collecting data about crime for the house of newspapers by whom I am employed, and in this book I have drawn liberally upon the two experiences.

First, a word about the title of this book. I have chosen it because the major part covers the period when I was Head of the Vice Squad, and it is when the lights of London begin to glow that the denizens of the underworld of vice engage in their nefarious trades, so *London After Dark* is an appropriate description of a good deal of what follows.

During my time with the Vice Squad I spent hours watching clubs, brothels, betting houses and other establishments of doubtful character. I got to know most of the "regulars" who paraded up and down my beat, and sometimes the gentlemen who "protected" them. To those who have had no first-hand knowledge of this kind of life it may appear romantic, but let me assure you from a long experience that it is sordid in the extreme. I have met a number of ordinary crooks who were quite likeable fellows, but I cannot remember a single individual behind organized vice whom I would not willingly have put away for a very long time. The average crook, excluding the stop-at-nothing gangsters, blackmailers, and such like, although on the wrong side of the law, have certain rough and ready standards, from which they seldom depart. The blackguards who traffic in dope or live on the immoral earnings of women, however, have no redeeming features—they are not only immoral but amoral.

A problem which has been exercising the minds of the general public in recent years is that of the homosexuals, and there is a danger that the serious nature of the offence may be underestimated. It is suggested in certain quarters, for instance, that what two adults do is entirely their own business, and the same kind of argument is applied to the perverts. If the results of their activities could be restricted to themselves, then there might be something to be said in favor of the argument, but as I shall show in the following pages, sexual perversion so often leads to other crimes, not the least of which are blackmail and sometimes murder. Whatever excuses are made for the individual, we must not blind ourselves to the fact that if vice is allowed to go unchecked it will destroy the moral stability of the whole nation.

During the past year or so I have visited some of my old haunts, and, as I am no longer serving, some places where I might not have been so welcome as I am today. Old crooks confide in me, the proprietors of shady concerns invite me in. I am a member of most of the "best" places, and some of the worst.

When my mind goes back over thirty years' service at Scotland Yard as a Detective Officer, I believe that my decision to treat crooks I would meet fairly and honestly has returned enormous dividends. Many I have "put away" have come to see me, not as you might think to "tap" me, but to tell me some little tid-bit of news which they think might help me. Recently I met an old lag who hailed me in the street, and with a puckish grin said: "Remember when you did me for so-and-so 'Guv'? Bit of a lark, wasn't it? Now it's all over I can tell you you missed some of the gear which we had parked." "Well, that's a fine thing," I replied, "and I told the Judge that I thought you had helped us as far as you were able." "It's all in the game," was the rejoinder.

One colored fellow brought a smile to my face only the other day when he came up to me and said: "Hello, boss, you 'member when you had a fight with John Margot in Bateman Street and when you beat him up, you no pinch and send him home in car?" "Yes," I said, "poor old John was a very silly boy." I refer to John Margot in this book. He was of as fine physique as I have ever seen for a colored man, and on the up and coming as a heavy-weight boxer, but Red Biddy and the girls got him down, till finally, in a fracas in a club, he received a slash across his left wrist which almost paralyzed his arm. In drink it would take six policemen to take him in. I had a great deal to do with colored fellows around Soho, and I found them easy to deal with if you told them the truth and played the game with them. They are like schoolboys, and even today I often see some of them, getting old, certainly, but not "very old," for you don't often see old colored folk in London. We talk of the time "he" was torpedoed, or "he" was bombed out, or when "he" received a decoration, or "him" that never came back from his trip.

Simple folk, believe me, but they so often get bad names

through the young trollops who become their "camp followers."

As a part of my present job I have made a number of tours of police forces throughout Great Britain, and discussed with detectives actually on the job some of their most interesting cases. A selection of these are included in this book, and I hope you will derive as much pleasure in reading about them as I did in recording them.

In conclusion, I am indebted to Kemsley Newspapers for permission to draw upon material acquired while engaged in the service of the Company.

LONDON AFTER DARK

Part One

LONDON AFTER DARK

London's Night Clubs

THAT DISTRICT OF LONDON KNOWN AS THE West End, and described by Her Majesty's Post Office as "London, W. 1," is roughly one mile square. It includes Piccadilly Circus and Leicester Square and all the little restaurants and clubs that form Soho, which is not so much an area you could mark out as an atmosphere that pervades part of the West End.

In the daytime, here are the most exclusive and among the most expensive shops in the world. There are hairdressers' establishments here, so elegant that upon great occasions of the Court, such as a Coronation, they distribute colored rosettes in strict order of rank to their dozens of waiting clients, purple for duchesses, red for baronesses, blue for mere baronets' wives, and so on.

There are jewelers' salons where ladies are told: "It will be quite simple to enlarge the tiara, madame—we still have the

diamonds that were removed from it for your grandmother—
what a tiny head she had!" And there are the tailors of Savile
Row—unchallenged as the best in the world, where a gentleman will still order a dozen suits from one roll of cloth, and
may drift pleasantly on for two or three years before con-
descending to remember to pay his bill, without making
anybody unhappy or apprehensive, for the probability is that
his family have been customers there since the reign of
George II.

There are restaurants such as Hatchetts, which used to be
a tavern cellar celebrated for its hot toddies and enormous
breakfasts by travelers waiting for the horse-drawn Express
Flying Coaches, and taverns that are not much changed from
the days when they sold tankards of sherry to Shakespeare
and Ben Jonson and gin by the flagon to Nell Gwynne's
roisterous friends.

After dark, these selfsame pavements cease to echo with
the ghostly footsteps of London's proud history and become
the wickedest pavements of England. The Square Mile of
Vice, we call it—Soho and the West End—where you can buy
anything and see everything—and where, in the right circumstances, you could get your throat slit more promptly than in
a pirate ship on the China Seas!

I know that Square Mile of Vice as well, I think, as any
living man on earth. When I was a young policeman at Scotland Yard, its pavements were the first beat I ever trod. After
almost a quarter of a century, I became Chief of London's
Vice Squad, and today there is nothing that could happen in
the West End of London which would surprise me . . . nothing
that has not happened before, in my experience.

For twenty-eight years the West End has been my office
table and workbench. The art of being a good policeman in a
metropolis like London consists of knowing everybody, and of
winning their friendship; so that when such situations arise as
the Hyde Park Jewel Robbery, it needs no painstaking Sherlock
Holmes work with magnifying glass on the carpet: one simply

knows that every skein and thread of the sensitive web that makes up the secret life of London will all lead back to you. In this well-known robbery four young socialites, whose families delved far back into the nobility, decided in a mood of greed and folly to lure a jeweler to the famous Hyde Park Hotel, where they had hired a suite in a false name. The plan was to hit him behind the ear with a cosh and steal his samples, worth about £30,000.

The four young fools did not realize that it is a skilled job to hit a man successfully behind the ear so that he promptly collapses. In London there are practitioners of violence like the Hymie Brothers, about whom I will tell you in this book, who could—when necessary—administer such a blow with the skill of a Harley Street surgeon. But they set a fee upon their illicit skill, and might ask up to £500 for performing that single dexterous wrist twist.

The Mayfair Boys, blundering, excited amateurs in a world of criminal adventure, struck at the jeweler and discovered, as so many other men have done, that the only result was, a terrifying splash of blood, a loud shriek from their intended victim, and a life-and-death struggle in which the cosh had to be used like a flail, until the unfortunate jeweler was smashed and beaten almost to the point of death.

His jewels were stolen, and the four badly frightened men scurried off into the jungle of the West End. Soon there was a voice on the telephone for me at one of my favorite bars:

"Mr. Fabian?" I recognized the husky voice of an underworld friend who specialized in receiving stolen property.

"Yes, Tad," I said. He told me: "I'm phoning just round the corner from the Salvo Club. There's four flash young geezers—look like right toffs—got some jewelry to sell, and want cash. One of them's got a bit of blood on his shirt-cuff. Looks dodgy to me, Guv'nor—I thought you'd like to know."

Within a few hours the four young Mayfair men were arrested, and later sentenced to heavy terms of imprisonment. Two received the cat—and a prison flogging is not a light matter, even when it falls upon the sturdy shoulders of a hardened East End thug.

But the significance of the story is that when Tad the Fence saw these four young men with the jewelry, he did not just do nothing about it: he telephoned me. One can hardly blame him for refusing to deal with them. Any astute villain would have realized that that jewelry was likely to be too hot for any kind of sane risk. Undoubtedly, if Tad had thought he could safely get away with it, he would have bought the stuff. But he had too much sense. So, he phoned his friend Fabian. He knew that if there was any reward coming from an insurance company, I would see that he got it without anybody necessarily knowing he had given me the information. He knew, too, that when next time it came my way to "feel his collar" for possessing stolen goods I would see that the judge was told: "This man is always very co-operative with the police, and has helped us materially in clearing up certain matters. . . ." Or something like that. The point being that Tad, and a thousand like him, knew me and knew he could—within the limits of the unwritten rules—trust me.

I did not make the acquaintance of these people from the *Police Gazette.* I got to know them in the haunts and dives where they spent most of their time, and their variously ill-gotten treasures.

Walking the streets of the West End—the murky ones as well as the bright ones—one felt, as I have frequently thought, like a gamekeeper who takes over an estate of crowded coverts and woodlands. One night you would walk down Frith Street, say, and everything would be exactly as it was the night before. Tomorrow there would be a new face on the corner—some pert, hard-eyed girl with a sexily painted mouth and slightly foreign look about her. You would stop and say: "We haven't met, have we?" And before she could reply, out of the adjacent shadows would glide her protector, who would naturally be standing near to look after her on her first few nights. "G'evening, Guv'nor," he would say, amiably if a bit apprehensively, "this is Ursula—she's a Polack. Ursula, this is Mr. Fabian, Chief of the Manor—you don't give him any nonsense, and he'll treat you fair."

Two or three more paces—and there is a glint of light from a cellar that tonight has thick curtains, and last night was bare. Another club that has sprung up, as a mushroom or a spotted purple toadstool might spring up suddenly in the middle of a woodland path where yesterday was a bare patch of moss. The West End is constantly changing—its faces and particularly its clubs, registered or unregistered, wink in and out like the lights of fireflies. So that, perhaps, no man can truthfully say: "I know everything and everybody in the West End of London" —but I can truthfully say, and I think it is the better boast: "All the West End of London knows me!"

As a young policeman I used to spend every Tuesday and Friday evening at the Polytechnic Boxing Club, and every Saturday afternoon that I could find free, in winter, on the rugger field. I never went in much for cricket. But all the rest of the time was devoted to my "jungle," the twin forests of Mayfair and Soho . . . and the winking, ephemeral lights of the night clubs and bars. One had to keep some of their secrets. A successful policeman must learn what he can tell and what he should keep to himself. There was, for instance, a secret exit from Kate Meyrick's notorious 43 Club in Gerrard Street, in the very house where Dryden lived from 1686-1700. During the time that I knew Kate and her club, it was paid several official "visits" by my police colleagues. The raiding parties never discovered about the back exit, which led through a courtyard beyond the outside toilets, and through an unlocked door of an adjoining shop's backyard, into the freedom of Newport Market. Many a patron—often very important names that might have caused a national scandal had they been caught in Kate's Club on a police raid, took advantage of the "exit." I did not see that it was any part of my business at that time to mention that I knew about it. I could rely upon Kate never to push anybody through the "escape hatch" who was better in the hands of the law!

The famous Kate Meyrick was a neat, stern little woman, who might easily have run a first-class seminary for well-brought-up young ladies. Nearly always she dressed in blacks or dark greys, and presided over the 43 Club from her little desk that was ensconced in a draft-proof cashier's box by the entrance.

You might think that if you came to a night club and paid the fantastic prices for cover-charges, champagne and cloak-room, the management might let you make a little whoopee if you felt in the mood. But Kate never permitted any nonsense from anybody. "Fun is fun," she would say firmly, "but vulgarity is vulgarity. Out you go, my boy!"

I remember once, in my earliest days, admiring the way she dealt with a gang of young "bloods" who burst into the little foyer. I was in plain clothes, of course, but at the sight of them I prickled, ready for trouble. They were in full evening dress with white carnations, obviously in from Oxford or Cambridge for a mad night, and already flushed with high spirits and drink. A moment later I had the surprise of my life—and learned another lesson about the strange ways of Soho's denizens. They straightened themselves and advanced upon Kate.

"Please, Ma'am," said the leader, humbly—and I recognized him as a marquis in his own right, while behind him stood the weedy but amiable heir to one of England's greatest dukedoms —"please let us in, Ma'am. We haven't got the ten bob each for admission . . . won't you let us in for half a crown each?"

Kate viewed them sternly. "Just this time, then," she said, "and you can owe me the half-crowns. But you don't stay longer than an hour, any of you—and the first sign of nonsense, out you all go!"

I could not help but think of the head waiters in London at that time who would gladly have given free suppers and the best champagne for the kudos of having that youthful group in their restaurants.

There was another night when a man arrived with a group of friends, and he was not short of half a crown. He was one of the most lavish spenders in London, and he, too, had a peerage. But Kate Meyrick halted him imperiously. "You do not come in here for one month, my lord," she said. "If I am not good enough to be acknowledged by you when we pass in Bond Street, I must teach you manners." And the Queen of Clubs, as London called her, turned away a certain profit of £40 or £50 with a whisk of her hand, and—you might have thought— had made an important enemy.

But a month later his lordship turned up again with another party, and a great bouquet of flowers for the straight-spined little old lady who ruled London's night life. One of her daughters married the Earl of Kinnoul.

There was a fortune made at the Hambone Club that appeared miraculously one night in Ham Yard from what had been a derelict premises huddled in a dark corner. Some genius transformed it into the appearance of an old-fashioned hostelry, and one had to climb three flights of stone stairs, sand-bestrewn, to reach the club. Upon each stairway a flunkey, in full wig, waited. The great, the rich and the infamous of London ascended those stairs, and nearly every night the little club was crowded to its 120 limit. Nobody ever received a cloakroom ticket for hats and coats, and nobody ever received the wrong garment! It was one of those small miracles of organization that help to build the reputation of a club. But the actual formula for success in the West End is as great a mystery as that for writing a popular song, or a best-selling novel. One man will spend £50,000 on decorating a single room, and within a month of the first ballyhoo of opening there is nothing but a bored orchestra, a dozen rebellious waiters, and a bailiff on the step.

And at the same time, a negro from nowhere, like Frisco,

can open up a poky little cellar, decorated with five pounds' worth of painted hessian and dried-up palm leaves, and become one of the great names of Europe as a club proprietor.

A few doors away from the 43 Club was the celebrated Big Apple, one of the best-known colored clubs in London. I had a great deal to do with the African and West Indian boys in the West End, and got along with them very well. You cannot tell me that they are an inferior race. I think that their behavior is a marvel of good humor, wit and sensitiveness, considering the handicaps with which most of them have to struggle, and although there are sinners among them they are no different from white men in that regard. There was an outstandingly good heavyweight negro boxer named John Margot, who was called "Senegal" for nickname, and would undoubtedly have been one of the finest fighters in the world had he been handled properly.

But like many another misunderstood genius, John became a little crazy with drink. He used to swallow Red Biddy (cheap red wine and methylated spirits) actually by the quart and gallon, and would go berserk. I saw six policemen unable to carry him out of some premises that he had successfully broken up. I went up to him and said quietly: "John, get up and be a gentleman. It's Mr. Bob speaking to you." I had to repeat this a couple of times, and then to the amazement of everybody he straightened himself, brushed himself down and walked chatting with me to the Police Station. I have known this to happen half a dozen times.

I learned all about jazz, boogie-woogie and calypso from my colored friends years before they became known outside the murky little "colored clubs." When we were all in the mood—which was often—I would persuade them to give me a "jam session" that would have opened new doors to any white musician, who had cared to spare the time to listen, in those days. I found that the African boys and myself shared a pleasure in boyish practical jokes—sneezing powder, a pin on a chair, rubber hammers, and so on. And there was one occasion when a colored man was "wanted" very badly for a villainous offense. He had simply disappeared from the West End and the police could not find him. I was being badgered by the "Upper Ten" at the Yard and I walked into one of my colored clubs and told them my troubles. "What'll happen if you don't find him, Mr. Bob?" I was asked. I replied, truthfully enough, that I might be removed to another district. They exchanged glances, and in a few hours I received a message: "That fellow—he's in Cardiff, and he signs at the Labor Exchange every Tuesday and Friday. . . ."

Another famous club in Ham Yard was run by Freddie Ford, and the last I heard of Freddie was that the hands which so capably served the finest champagne and caviar in Ham Yard were now serving—with no less deftness—fish and chips at a super supper bar just behind Shaftesbury Avenue! But in his clubland days Freddie Ford was a very potent name indeed. I've no idea where he came from, but it was probably from the East End. He had the appearance and manner of a Guards Brigade colonel, with big military moustache, ruddy complexion, oxen shoulders and straight back.

Freddie's chief claim to fame, I think, was the way he simply flouted the licensing laws, without the slightest attempt at covering up. When he was raided and fined, he just went on doing it. "Fines are part of my business expenses," he used to say.

Next door to the Big Apple was the night club known as "Hell." It was run by Geoffrey Daybell and was probably best known as the favorite haunt of Sam Henry, a gargantuan Jewish business man who made a fortune out of supplying liquor and wines to the West End clubs. Sam Henry began his business career with a tiny shop in Dean Street, Soho, where he sold ladies' underwear, and went on to become head waiter at the Shim-Sham Club in Wardour Street. Next, he bought an off-license shop in Wardour Street, and that was the first of his astute business moves. Sam never made a mistake, and died worth a fortune. But he was a kindly, generous and well-loved man. I suspect that many a "pension" died with him, and that poverty came suddenly and starkly back to many a helpless man and woman who had been on Sam's private list of dependents. I suppose he may be said to have drunk himself to death, although with such a gay and popular man it is inaccurate to make a suggestion that he would ever deliberately destroy himself. It was just that Sam's bulky personage could not stir abroad in the West End without being pressed to share hospitality at this table—at that table—at this bar and that club . . . he was drinking about three bottles of brandy and three bottles of champagne every day until shortly before he was buried in the Jewish Cemetery, with half London, myself included, as his mourners.

The Hell Club, where Sam spent a good deal of his time, was installed with hidden lighting that changed color slowly, at a time when this was quite a novelty, and sank from pink to deep red and into ghastly purple, and with various effects to make flickering shadows. I have no doubt that some of the patrons must have thought they had actually arrived!

It was the invention of the "bottle party" that helped to make the fortune of Sam Henry, although the idea was not his own.

The bottle party was invented by that singularly astute brain in the distinguished—and now gray—head of Eustace Hoey. Eustace Hoey at one time owned the off-license shop in Warwick Street, also one in Rupert Street. He studied the licensing laws very carefully, and came to the awareness that there was nothing to prevent a delivery being made at any time or place to the client of a wine shop who ordered in licensing hours. In fact, and to put it more simply, if you were a client of the Wine Store, there was nothing to prevent you from telephoning Mr. Hoey from the gaudy premises of, say, the Shim-Sham club and ordering a bottle of champagne to be delivered to your table!

As the law—embarrassed and desperate—dodged and side-stepped with fresh clauses to rid itself of this thorn in its side,

Eustace Hoey coolly and cleverly followed each change in the
Act with a variation of approach! It was a memorable battle—
a clean fight on both sides; and when the licensing laws finally
sounded the death-knell of the bottle party, Eustace Hoey
retired gracefully without dishonor.

Today he owns the celebrated and irreproachable Ward-
room Club in Curzon Street which bears his hallmark—of
exceptionally good *décor,* mostly carved oak panelling, furniture and curtains of the best, and china, cutlery, napery fit for
a baronial hall—which is, indeed, where much of it comes
from! He has also recently taken over the famous Bristol Grill.

Another colossus of London's club life is Jack Olivieri, now
proprietor of the Celebrity Restaurant in Clifford Street and
the Galleon Club in Victoria Street. He has owned the Knightsbridge Studio Club, the famous Esquire in Piccadilly, and has
had interests in the Strangers in St. James, the Unity in
Jermyn Street. . . .

It is a balancing act to be marvelled at, this feat of running
a chain of successful clubs in the West End. You must be so
tough that the gangsters will respect you and let you prosper
in peace, so smooth and urbane that you can collect clients
from the pages of Debrett around you, worldly enough to
attract the hard business men, tolerant enough to be in sympathy with all the strange flotsam and mixed morals that are
as inevitable in the West End as seaweed on the shore, and
you must have the knowledge of a showman, the skill of a
maître d'hôtel—and luck in huge slices. With all this, if you can
get a good chef and persuade him to stay, a good head waiter
who will not let the waiters rob you . . . it seems like easy
money, but it is to be made only by the type of man who
could run a successful South American revolution as well as a
luxury hotel!

I remember the sumptuous Lambs Club over Leicester
Square Tube Station when I raided it on January 21, 1924. It
presented several problems, for the only entrance was by way
of a lift from the hallway of an entrance in Cranbourn Street.

There was no stairway up at all. The doorman was an astute gentleman who received a very large salary to keep an alert lookout, and you had to be personally known to him before you could ever hope to get near to the lift without him pressing the alarm button.

Inside this fortress, upon a superb maple floor that came from the then Prince of Wales's private ranch in Alberta, the sons and daughters of Debrett, with a wonderful sprinkling of the famous and the notorious, used to enjoy themselves in what they apparently fancied was immunity from the Acts which deal with the sale and consumption of liquor.

The plan decided upon was that a bevy of stout constables in plain clothes—with some in uniform—should be handily waiting around the corner of Cranbourn Street, while another officer and myself had the task of getting into that lift before the quick-witted doorman pressed the button that would not merely immobilize it, but would sound the clangor upstairs, upon which signal every scrap of evidence would be immediately swallowed and the glasses rinsed out with soda-water or ginger ale.

We conceived a scheme. And on the night of the raid we pulled up at Lambs Club in a taxi, going through the motions of being ever so slightly flushed by alcohol. The doorkeeper watched, unimpressed, as we had our little *argument* about who should pay the taxi. I had a handful of money, and my colleague, striving to snatch my sleeve for the privilege of paying off the taxi, spilt it on the pavement. The sight of those half-crowns and shillings rolling about was too much for the doorkeeper, who emerged from his watch tower to assist me in picking them up.

He was promptly seized, bundled into the taxi and sat upon firmly while the steady tramp of outsize boots sounded around the corner as the first contingent of raiders packed themselves into the lift!

The Quadrant Club in Regent Street was another gilded box that offered difficulties to the would-be raider. The club stood on the corner of one of the arcades, and the security measures were almost impregnable—or so the proprietors must have thought.

At this time, in May 1924, Regent Street was being rebuilt, and the job had been given to me, as a test of ingenuity, to lead a raiding party into this club. I climbed up the steel shell of the nearest building under reconstruction, and across the adjoining roof, until I reached the fanlight of the Quadrant Club, with colleagues close behind me. It was a warm evening, and we had presumed that the fanlight would be slightly ajar. We were correct in this assumption—it was opened by about three inches. But it was securely fixed by a staple through the adjusting bar. As I bent down to try to unfix his bar, my foot slipped on the green mold of the roof, and I crashed through the glass of the fanlight, hung poised for an instant upon some thick drapery that covered the ceiling, and then fell flat upon my back on the floor of the ladies' cloakroom. All the wind was knocked out of me, and both my hands were very badly gashed and bleeding from where I had grabbed at the shattered fanlight to break my fall.

Fortunately there was no shriek. The ladies' room was empty of anybody but me.

"You all right?" demanded a voice from the fanlight. My two fellow officers were peering anxiously down. "All right," I said. "Give the signal that I'm just about to go downstairs and open the door!"

I opened the door of the ladies' room, and on the stairs, presumably to investigate the crash which they had mistaken for a burglar, were two of Quadrant's burliest waiters. I must have looked an unattractive sight, rumpled, cut and bloodsplashed.

They came for me like a couple of Hollywood thugs, and I could not clench my fists. But I had often seen the negro wrestler Black Butcher Johnson turn to grasp the ropes and kick out at his opponent. It would have done him good that night to see his pupil. I caught one waiter with each foot while holding on to the doorknob of the ladies' powder room, and they went tumbling down the carpeted stairs in a heap. A pair of West End playboys in evening dress looked up, astonished, and then must have recognized that it was a police raid, for they both smiled, and one drawled: "Well done, Robert!" They obligingly blocked a flying wedge of waiters that was approaching.

There was a little pub in Air Street, where Swan and Edgars now stands, where the Bright Young Things of the Gay 'Twenties splashed vintage champagne. A part of the shop that is now Austin Reeds used to be the Chinese Restaurant presided over by the prince of London's dope smugglers and white-slave traffickers, the infamous Brilliant Chang.

There were other clubs in Ham Yard where hardly a night passed without some robbery or violent assault, and the Empire Club underneath the Criterion where a man named Unfreville died suddenly. The first place in Britain where reefer cigarettes—marijuana—were smoked was in the Nest Club in Kingly Street, and there was the Billiards Hall in Wardour Street where you could see wonderful fights any night.

But it's just the same in London today, although the names have changed and the faces are different—new faces and the same ones but older. Night life goes on. . . .

One night, as I descended the lamplit steps that lead down into fashionable Curzon Street, built over the site of Lansdowne House, a girl hurried from the night shadows towards me.

She was young, slender as a cornstalk, and her hair as yellow. She used the railing as footrest, and adjusted the ankle-strap of her pencil-heel shoe. Her eyes watched me.

Her leg would have looked better in school socks, I thought, than tight, glimmering nylons. When you have worked twenty-eight years at Scotland Yard you do not blush at a glimpse of a girl's knee.

"Late for a kid like you—larking about in a street like this, isn't it?"

She smiled. "I'm looking for a bit of excitement," she said, "aren't you?"

Before I could reply, she added: "I'm not One of Those!" She said this firmly and proudly, with a ring of truth in it.

"What kind of excitement, then?"

"Oh—music—dancing—some place to go when everywhere else is shut—you know . . ."

Yes, indeed, I knew. In the headquarters of Scotland Yard's Vice Squad is a big black book—well-thumbed—the only copy of its kind in the world. It is called "The Clubs Book." It is the policeman's private guide to London night life. I helped to write it.

There are 295 registered clubs within one mile of Eros Statue in Piccadilly Circus. Deeper in shadow, behind Leicester Square and up to Goodge Street, are fifteen unregistered clubs at present known to the police. A total of 310 places, ablaze with lights and activity into London's dawn, where music, dancing, drinks and companions await the well-filled wallet. The job is to empty that wallet—whether they do it with pink champagne and satin-quilted walls; or by meths-and-ginger-ale, marijuana cigarettes and dope-jumpy 'teen-age girls who, for £2 would cuddle a baboon.

The girl was watching my face. "D'you know any night clubs?" she asked. She couldn't quite size me up.

"Not many," I lied. In my pocket at that instant were forty-seven membership cards to London's night clubs. I am also honorary member of fifty more. But I am never too proud to learn.

"Well," said the girl eagerly, "I know a nice little friendly club, just around the corner from here—it's not a boozy place, but there's music—an' girls . . ."

The club was up back stairs, over a shop behind Curzon Street. It was just one room. The floor was bare and held half a dozen rickety tables with green wooden chairs. The whole lot looked as if they'd been borrowed from a public park.

The "bar" was a trestle table, across one corner, covered with green baize and a few strips of tinsel. The barman, a husky villain about forty, in soiled lumberjacket shirt, gave a sickly grin when he saw me.

"Why, hullo, Guv'nor!" His eye jerked guiltily around his little club. Its occupants were four 'teen-age trollops, and half a dozen gloomy, provincial-looking men of various ages, who sat there in strained silence.

"There's nothing dodgy here, you know—we don't sell nothing but soft drinks, Mr. Fabian—don't need no club license for that!" He was addressing me, but his glance was upon my fair-haired young companion. It could have slain her. She tossed her head insolently. "How the hell was I to know?" she said, and reached for a cigarette. Her fingers trembled.

"Now, now, Cliff," I said, "you know I'm not in the police these days. I just came up to see an old friend."

Cliff's thick lips widened at once. "Straight, Guv'nor? For a minute I thought we'd had it!" He reached for a tumbler. "Have a drink, Mr. Fabian—not this muck!"—he gestured at the rows of bottles, charged with red, green or yellow fluid. "I've some decent stuff in the kitchen."

"What are those?" I pointed at the bottles. "The usual fruit cocktails? A mixture of citric acid, dye and barley water, in small glasses at five shillings each?"

"Seven-an'-sixpence, Guv," attested Cliff without shame. "The kids here—like Lucy—get a tosh—a half-crown—on each drink, and the management—that's me—gets the other five bob."

Lucy stared at me, a cigarette dangling from her lips, one young eye screwed up where the smoke from it was bothering her. "You're wise to this joint, then?" she said, in 'teen-age imitation American.

"I think so," I said. "Smart villains like Cliff get half a dozen girls like you to haunt milk bars, night cafes and street corners, and look for likely mugs. Foreigners, provincials, young men on the spree. You promise something between the

Moulin Rouge and the Garden of Allah, and bring 'em up
here. Then you persuade them to buy 'fruit cocktails' for you
and themselves, just as fast as they can be swallowed."

"Faster the better," said Lucy. "They taste terrible!" She
grimaced, and for that instant, looked heart-renderingly
childlike.

"How do the customers stand for it?" I asked, and I really
wanted to know.

Lucy smiled, slowly. "They don't! When they've paid for
three or four rounds, fifteen bob a time, and nothin's happened, they get cheesed and blow." She tossed her beautiful
head. "If they cut up nasty, Cliff sorts them out. Then we go
out and round up another lot!"

"How much d'you make in a night, Lucy?"

Lucy pouted thoughtfully. "Maybe a fiver a night, week-
days, and twice as much Saturdays an' Sundays."

"She's a liar," said Cliff amiably. "You have to excuse her,
Mr. Fabian. Many a night the kids don't make more'n a quid
or thirty bob. They like to talk big. Call themselves 'night club
entertainers' and 'dance hostesses' to their pals, an' boast
something sickening when they get back in the remand homes.
So the word gets around, and we get plenty kids to pick from."

"Some of these girls are a bit young, aren't they?" I asked
accusingly.

Cliff shrugged. "Well, Mr. Fabian—you know how it is
with kids these days. Tougher'n we are, some of 'em. We get
the zombies (policewomen) around here with the Children's
Waggon pretty often—but it's easy to pick up another lot."

Lucy sniffed, and strolled over to one of the tables where
the young men were seated, hunched gloomily on their elbows.

"Like to buy me a drink, bud?" I heard her say, as she
perched on the table's rickety edge. A spasm of dismay flitted
across the boy's face. He could hardly have been twenty. "Oh,
er—all right," he said weakly, and fumbled in his pocket.

Twenty-three London clubs were raided and prosecuted
last year. Eight were struck off the register. Four other un-

savory clubs were stamped on by the police before they even got their first customer in. In the Metropolitan Police district there are actually two clubs for every five public houses— 2,877 clubs. They are all under hawklike supervision—even places patronized by Royalty.

During a raid on Churchill's Club in New Bond Street, a police inspector and a "zombie," posing as revelers, saw whiskies served after three a.m., when the club's license went up to two-thirty a.m. only.

Here, in rooms padded like expensive chocolate-boxes— even the ceilings draped with pleated satin—theatre folk, Debrett, journalists, stockbrokers, jockeys—and members of the Royal Family—pay table fees of £1 each to be greeted by a head waiter (£30 a week) and see a cabaret (nearly £200 a night). The white-capped chef earns £30 a week. Members of Churchill's have their own drinking goblets, with names engraved on one side, and Churchill's saucy coat-of-arms on the other. Playboy-swindler Eddie Crane had one.

Dapper Harry Meadows (whose moustache rivals comedian Jimmy Edwards') runs Churchill's . . . the 21 Club . . . and La Rue's—where Princess Margaret has a favorite balcony table. Such clubs as these . . . Jack Olivieri's "Celebrity" . . . Bobby Barnett's "Embassy" and "400 Club" . . . are for London's champagne and orchids trade. The police has also raided the exclusive Albany Club, on Savile Row, next door to the tailoring shop where King George V had his suits made, and where all the officers of the Guards Brigade and Household Cavalry go. Distinguished patronage does not spare London's clubs from police raids.

All around the Windmill Theatre are sprinkled the more Bohemian night clubs.

Best of these is probably Club Panama, run by Harry Adams, Napoleon of Night Clubs, who has owned a large number of clubs in London and entertained, among countless others, the Duke of Windsor, Kreuger the match-millionaire and Haigh the acid-bath murderer.

Night closes over London, and, under the light of a lamp, two people meet

Walls keep their secrets in a typical London alley

Drama or romance?

Outside a London pub, "hot dogs" find ready customers; for those who prefer a restaurant, Soho provides for every taste

For some, life begins after dark; for others,
like the kids below, it's time to go home to bed

Edgar Manning, described as "the worst man
in London," was the dope king of his time

Brilliant Chang, who is reputed to
have made £1,000,000 out of dope

I spend much of my time wandering round odd spots in London

It was in the old Club Panama that Neville Heath met Marjorie Gardner, the girl he tortured and murdered. Dancing girls trot and caper on the dance floor, then sit at supper tables. If customers wish to dance with them, they usually can. "We don't force anybody," says Harry.

It is my belief that Harry Adams is the outstanding character today in London's club life. He has owned so many clubs that a list of them would be bewildering. I think he started with Moody's Club just after the last war. These days you can always tell an Adams Club—like an Adams fireplace—for Harry decorates them himself, and he is an excellent artist. His favorite motif is a mural scene of palm-trees, sands and blue seas. He also has one of the most knowledgeable eyes in London for theatrical talent, and there is many a promising name in the entertainment world today that started on the small cleared floor space between the tables of one or other of Harry's clubs. He is a little man, Jewish, with a good-tempered face and an inexhaustible fund of comical Jewish stories, mostly with the laugh against himself. His favorite method of talking business is to think of a good idea, seek out among his innumerable friends the right man to bring it into existence, and then say: "Well, there's the idea—do what you like with it!" Strangely, even among the marble-cold hearts of the West End, this method works—for Harry, if for nobody else. He is a man who could write a book about London's night life, if anybody could. I think he has had every celebrity in London, in his Club, at some time or another.

Within a few yards of the Club Panama is the Be-Bop Club, with dance license until four a.m., where the only drink is ginger-wine at half-crown a glass or coffee, and the floor show is provided by contortions of the dancers themselves. This is an unregistered club. Others, much more sinister, lurk not far away.

A burly African guards the notorious, unregistered Twilight Club, back of Gerrard Street. His nose has been knuckle-sculptured into potato-shape. Two tall, polite young negroes run the club. The main room is like an underground ware-house. At little tables, forty to sixty members sit, drink black coffee from tiny cups (1s. each), Coca-cola or ginger beer. Some eat thick sandwiches. Most are negroes. And some are young white girls.

The air is prickly with smoke. As soon as you cough, every eye is upon you, suspiciously. You have betrayed yourself. It means your throat is new to the dry tickle of marijuana cigar-ettes—reefers, giggle-smoke, love-weed, bhang, ganji, Indian hay—call it any name you like, it is hemp tobacco, potent with hashish. It hangs in the air like the taste of sin.

Across the room, a band plays bewitching rhythms. The musicians, dark and absorbed, have eyes half-shut. The pianist is a white boy, pale as a death-mask, his sensitive mouth like a wound waiting to bleed. When he wants to leave the piano, the big African drummer, or the fierce little Barbadian sax-player, lead him gently, patiently by the elbow, as if he were a sick child. He plays into his own darkness. Out of it come the plummy, hot-chocolate voices of the dancers, the chirrupy giggles of their pitifully young girl friends.

It is not the fault of the colored boys that this is one of the most dangerous clubs in London. They seek company of their own kind. There exists in London not a single recreational hostel for negroes. They suck reefer cigarettes in clenched fists —to them as sinful as whisky was sinful to New Yorkers in pro-hibition days, as black market eggs were sinful to us.

They have brains of children, can only dimly know the cruel harm they do to the 'teen-age girls who dance with them and try thrilled puffs at those harmless-looking, crude pungent marijuana cigarettes.

Sipping coffee, not talking much, the real villains, the pimps—white men as often as not—sit and watch. Tomorrow or the next day, the gay negro escort, proud and excited by his young white girl companion, will go broke. The girl will awake, with eyeballs throbbing as if thumbs pressed them, lips slack and body quivering, for need of the marijuana cigarette that is not there.

Then the pimp sidles up to her and says softly: "I can get them for you—at a price. . . ."

Of all forms of drug-taking and dope-peddling that have infiltrated into London, this new marijuana menace is becoming the worst and most diabolical in the history of metropolitan crime!

SOMETIMES THROUGH THE THRONG OF Piccadilly's night traffic comes one of the Royal cars, with either the Queen herself or her sister Princess Margaret: the former bound for some theatre, the latter maybe an occasional night club. If it is for supper somewhere, the place is discreetly chosen, and the table a quiet one. But the Royal ladies are never alone for a moment in London after dark. The task of guarding them is one of the many duties of Scotland Yard.

I know very well the man who had, for twenty-two years, the task of acting as day-and-night bodyguard to the late King. With a compact black automatic pistol under his left armpit— never once did he find need to draw it, for the King was a greatly loved man—Chief Superintendent Hugh Cameron was the monarch's lanky, constant shadow.

He rode in the front seat of the Daimler limousine, and was always first out to open the door. Cameron's unflurried and rather cool glance surveyed the crowd for the two or three vital seconds that were all the time he ever had—or all he needed—to ensure the King's safety. He is a deadly shot.

For two years after he could have retired upon full police pension, Hugh Cameron continued to guard the King. When His Majesty died, the resignation papers of Cameron followed very quickly.

The responsibility—and distinction—of guarding Queen Elizabeth is now that of an athletic, quick-eyed youngish inspector who was not too long ago merely P.C. 264 "Nobby" Clarke in "C" Division of the Metropolitan Police. He has been an inspector now for only five years.

His real name is Thomas Clarke, and he is a tall, dark, self-effacing officer who was chosen to be the new Queen's bodyguard only a few months ago, after it had been discovered that her former guard (Inspector Alec Usher) had a slight physical disability that made it impossible for him to accompany Her Majesty and the Duke of Edinburgh in an airplane.

I used to live with Clarke, in the police section-house at Beak Street, but even though he was my colleague I neither noticed nor discovered much about him. His complete self-effacement was remarkable.

Clarke, in his quiet self-withdrawal, is typical of the men who walk unobtrusively in the footsteps of Britain's Royal Family. With only one exception they are surprisingly similar in appearance.

They are tall men, rather like cavalry officers, but none have moustaches or any distinguishing marks. They are quiet, uncommunicative, and long before they are appointed to the highly-prized posts of Royal bodyguards, they are watched by their police superiors for steadiness, punctuality, deadly calm in emergency.

Usually they are not noted for their humor, although one particularly outstanding exception is Inspector Frank Kelly, who guards the Duke of Edinburgh, and will continue to do so.

The Duke and Kelly have frequently been observed to exchange smiles at some little human incident that nobody else in the Royal party may have noticed.

The bodyguards are not Special Branch men, nor Security Service (M.I.5). They are all picked from the uniformed branch of the Metropolitan Police, and put into "A" Division, inside the Yard itself. They have private offices in Buckingham Palace, windows overlooking the rear courtyard, and a green telephone with secret "scramble" device fixed to it, to defeat eavesdroppers.

The only man who does not have his office in Buckingham Palace is Inspector Chisholm, who guards the Duke and Duchess of Gloucester. He has offices and apartments at York House. He is a bachelor, a distinguished police athlete, and has that typical air of calm detachment that seems to go with the task of being "personal detective to Royalty."

When they go to Ascot, these Royal guardians wear grey topper and morning dress. For theatres and evening occasions, they wear white tie and tails or dinner jackets, according to the strict demands of etiquette. They get an extra police allowance to cover costs of wardrobe, and expense items, such as: "laundry of dress-shirts, 2s." or "new grey cravat, two guineas."

These expenses are submitted to Chief Inspector A. E. Perkins, bodyguard to the Queen Mother, and now senior since the retirement of Hugh Cameron. Expenses are cleared through "A" Division Police Fund grant.

It is now twenty-three years since the tall, straight figure of Hugh Cameron walked for the first time up the wide stairs of No. 145, Piccadilly, into the private study of the man who was then Duke of York and destined to become King.

During all those subsequent years, Cameron went everywhere with the King. Mostly he wore a black jacket, striped morning trousers, stiff white collar and dark tie, like any senior member of the Royal Household.

When His Majesty went to Sandringham to shoot, it was Hugh Cameron's privilege to take his own holidays, if he chose. But nearly always he preferred to ask to go to Sandingham with the King. Towards the end, the two men had become such close friends that even when the King's personal shooting party was only four guests, Hugh Cameron was among them.

Chief Inspector A. E. Perkins is a graying-haired man, married, with no family, but a hobby for studying foreign languages.

The men who guard the Royal Family have little time for hobbies, or for private life. They are all men to whom the honor of their job is their main compensation. Everyone I have spoken to tells me that he gets the most courteous consideration from his Royal charges, who frequently go out of their way to say: "I shall stay in all morning and you do not need to worry about me until two o'clock."

When Princess Margaret went to theatres, parties and night clubs in the West End, young Inspector Jack Ashbrooke, D.F.C., has always been within a few feet of her. When she sat at small tables with her chosen friends, Ashbrooke, with his pistol and unwinking surveillance, was always near. He is a bachelor and lives in a police flat in Westminster.

The next interesting appointment will be the bodyguard for the young Duke of Cornwall, who should—unless his tastes are very unusual—be as keenly intrigued by the excitements and events of London's West End as any other young man becomes.

A JEWISH BUSINESS MAN WHO IS A VERY astute and successful dealer, and a good husband as well as being an honest man, was confessing to me over a drink at La Rue's that he had just lost £300 that day on the horse racing and was going to a gambling club—or "spieler" as they are called in the Metropolitan Police and thieves' slang—to try to recoup his losses.

"My luck can't stay bad all day, Bob," he said. I looked at him hard. "You are a mug, David," I said. "You are a very big mug indeed. Why a man as clever as you must dribble away his money on gambling, I can never understand."

He laughed without shame. "Bob," he said, "the thing is that when you win—it's tax-free!"

That is perhaps the main attraction about gambling, and there is always a boom in gaming in the West End when taxation is high. And of course the villains are in it, as usual. If you would like to win £1,000 on the turn of a card, or gam-

ble £5 a time at roulette and see the croupier push £175 winnings towards your fingers within twenty-five seconds of spinning his wheel . . . you can find all these things easily enough
in London, any night. There is no need to go to Le Touquet
or Monte Carlo. The only thing is, that when you do this in
London you are a criminal. Most gamblers don't seem to
realize this. They understand that the man who stages the game
is a criminal. But so are they, for playing!

The members of the theatrical profession, and film execu-
tives, are among the worst offenders. I visited a gambling party
recently, in the heart of Mayfair, that did not seem to be in
the least bit concerned that the regulations were being cracked
wide open.

But that, perhaps, was because the usual careful precautions had been taken.

The occupants of the flat—a West End furrier and his wife
—were spending the night at the Savoy Hotel, in one of the
expensive suites overlooking the Thames. They could afford to
—they had been paid £100 in cash (no income-tax) for the use
of their flat for one night!

The game shifts every night to a new address. The people
who had the gamblers on Wednesday will be the last people
in London to know where to find the game on Thursday.

Nor do they usually wish to know. The stakes are terrifying.

I saw a theatrical producer lose £600 on a single hand of
chemin-de-fer. I watched a fairly well-known jockey drop
£1,400 in the same game. A man who owns several restaurants
won a sum of money that he told me contentedly, was "just
a few quid under three grand, Bob!"

"Why d'you do it!" I said. "Why risk your money in a place
like this? You weren't a gambler before the war, I remember."

He twisted the thin stem of his brandy glass. "Well, Bob—
before the war gambling was a mug's game all right. If you
had a few quid—a bit of capital—you built it up until you had
enough to retire and live like a gentleman." He laughed, a bit
self-consciously.

"But with today's taxes there's almost no way a man can get his hands on a large chunk of capital except by gambling, football pools, or—this!"

"You could sell your restaurants," I said.

"No, Bob, while I'm in business I can get tax allowances. But if I sell out, and invest the capital in securities, I'm taxed at unearned income rates."

It is this slant that today is sending many of London's top-money men in search of these gaming parties where stakes run high.

We were on the second floor of a block of luxury flats in a beautifully furnished apartment. The boukhara rugs had been rolled up, away from the cigar-ash. The big, polished refectory table was covered by protecting asbestos pads and a green baize cloth. Piled in one corner of the biggest bedroom were all the *objets d'art* of the household, barricaded in by two silk tapestry sofas, out of harm's way.

The electric light bulbs in the chandeliers had been replaced by high-wattage, anti-glare blue lamps. A full-sized, professional roulette wheel occupied the largest table. This wheel had been smuggled up to the flat inside a large leather *pouffe* footstool. It weighed nearly seventy pounds.

The "chemmy" game occupied the drawing-room, and in the paneled hallway lounge was the poker-game, for the grimmest stakes of all.

Four uniformed flunkeys (£4 a night and keep-your-mouth shut) served drinks and refreshments, ordered from a West End caterer's. A white-capped chef (£6 a night, etc.) attended the buffet. There were two trolleys of *hors d'oeuvres,* and sparkling ice-bins for the wines.

For, while the games are on, refreshments are free. Champagne, chickens, turkeys, a flank of smoked salmon, Turkish, French and American coffee, a cabinet of cigars and cigarettes —everything free.

When the furrier and his wife returned, next day, all would

be tidied and replaced. A couple of bottles of best champagne would be left in the 'fridge, and perhaps a carton of caviar, a plateful of canapés, from the night's party. Only a few dents in the thick pile of the fitted carpets would show where many chairs had been tilted and scraped feverishly.

The men who organize these parties can afford to be generous.

I know (just as the police know) that there are two men in London today who run these parties regularly, and another two or three dozen who stage gambling parties frequently enough to have their own faithful clientele.

The organizer takes ten per cent of table stakes. When you change £1,000 notes into roulette-plaques or poker chips, you get £900-worth. As the roulette wheel spins, the organizer gets every stake when the number Zero or Double-Zero comes up. Also some of these men—not the top two operators—encourage card-sharps, who usually pay forty per cent of their winnings, plus about £100 "entrance fee."

In the Black Museum at Scotland Yard is a gadget we captured during a Flying Squad raid on a gambling party. It is a delicate instrument of wires, springs and pulleys, almost as small as the works of a watch. It fits the fore-arm, and strings run down to the left foot.

A card-sharp can, by a slight movement of his foot, under the table, operate this device—called a "hold-out"—and whisk a chosen card out of sight up his sleeve, at a speed the eye cannot possibly follow. When he wants to play this "stolen" card, he moves his foot, and the card is flipped into his hand.

Marked cards are not used in big games. Any experienced gambler—and all good police officers—can detect them at once, by the method known as "The £100 Secret." You pick up the pack, and riffle it with your thumb, the backs towards you. If there is any slight variation of the pattern, it immediately comes to life under your eyes, and seems to squirm and dance like a motion picture.

You can buy marked cards in London at conjurors' shops, for 5*s.* to £3, according to quality. But they are for novices only. The big-money cheats actually mark the cards while in play!

The marking is done by a smear of "daub," which is a crayon-like paste made by mixing a little printers' ink with stearine and wax, to which you add a few drops of Venetian turpentine. One West End card-sharper conceals the daub on his waxed moustache, and fingers it thoughtfully in play.

On the glossy back of a playing card the pale, greenish-gold daub leaves markings that can be seen only as the cards are tilted at an angle to the light. You can glimpse it like the second color in shot-silk, and only then if you are alertly looking for it.

The big-time gamblers of London are mostly men. There were about forty at this party, and only eight women. All the women but one played roulette for £1 stakes. The exception was a South American woman, playing *chemin-de-fer* and losing, as far as I could judge, about £200.

How do we find these games?

First thing we do is drop in for a drink at one of half a dozen respectable bars in the West End. In each of these nearly every night is a man who will tell the carefully guarded addresses. There are no passwords. If he knows you, he will tell you. If he doesn't know you, he won't. It is as plain as that.

Slightly lower down the "social scale," are the double-rummy packs for surprisingly high stakes. And at the bottom are the dice-games in cellars, back rooms of night clubs, over garages—even on Thames river-boats!

At these games, cheating is common. You can buy "loaded" dice at almost any novelty shop. They are not, these days, weighted with lead shot. They are slightly tapered. You can detect this by placing the two dice together, and match them up for size, on each side.

The dice-cheat doesn't use these himself. He lets you roll them. They are designed to lose. This is good psychology. If he

made lucky throws, you would be suspicious. But if his luck
varies, and yours is bad, he will win, just the same.

There are cheating put-and-take tops. You spin them left
for take and right for put; or else the spinning handle shifts
slightly up or down. Cheats can buy these tops for a few
shillings.

But it is not over these comparatively trivial gamblers that
the police are most worried. The big, luxury gamesters are the
real danger. Gambling is against the law. But it is not a crime
that most men feel indignant about. Most people gamble to
some extent every week.

The real harm is done when bribery of the police is attempted. The police know how quickly corruption, vice and
graft can follow in the wake of the gambler!

There is a gang in London that specializes in a certain form
of robbery by false pretenses, involving a gaming-den, and
the set-up must be unique in crime annals, if only for the
reason that every gamester around the tables loses all his
money to them, each time they work their swindle.

It is the usual sort of spieler, with a game of faro under
way, and two or three games of double-pack rummy; behind a
slight screen is a table for *chemin-de-fer*. The players are
generally theatricals, business men from the provinces, very
often Jewish, for this ordinarily shrewd and hard-working race
has an almost laughable weakness for gambling.

Suddenly there is a rush along the outside corridor, the
door is flung open, and five or six plain clothes officers burst
into the room. The occupants are paralyzed with shock and
apprehension. One of the raiding-party—presumably the inspector—calls: "Will you please keep your seats!" His men go
to each table, confiscate all the cards, the chips, any dice or
card-shoes or whatever other apparatus is on display. Also,
they pick up the money, take the names and addresses of
everybody, make each man empty his pockets and put the
assorted contents into a large manilla envelope, for which each
victim solemnly receives a receipt. Then the "inspector" has a

few words with the organizer of the gaming, and explains that
on this occasion the people will not be arrested, but that in a
few days they must expect to receive a summons for various
offenses under the gaming laws.

Yes, in cold print it is quite easy to guess what has happened. Nobody hears any more of it. The men were not police
officers—they are nearly all Irishmen, and their leader is a
Newcastle man who has spent the last twenty years in London
—when he was not in Parkhurst!

The best place in London for a legitimate gamble is the
White City dog track, where you can sit in the restaurant or
enclosure bar and enjoy some of the best food or drink in the
city, and place your bets on each race as it comes up, without
ever needing to bother your head to look at the track unless
you care to do so. It is the nearest thing in London to a lawful
casino. If you must gamble . . . and it seems unfortunate but
true that many people must! . . . then that is the place for you.
Stay out of the spielers, for if they don't take it from you one
way, they will find others. Many otherwise inexplicable robberies with violence are the result of collusion between the
proprietor of a gambling house in London, and a couple of
strong-arm gangsters—who accost the successful gamesters as
soon as they are safely away from the premises.

THE FIRST DRUG TRAFFICKER I EVER MET was Eddie the Villain, and I shall never forget him because it also happened to be my first week on duty as a policeman. I was a uniformed constable, with the white-and-blue armlet on my left wrist to indicate to the world that I was on my beat and not entitled to smoke, gossip or loiter. A police officer old enough to be my father was showing me around. He was due to retire in a few months, and all that mixed-up backyard of Soho, which had been his life for so many years, was just about to become mine, in his place.

We walked down Lisle Street, and my companion paused, drawing me into the shadows, as a tall, slim negro came out of a house. He was superbly well dressed—perhaps somewhat overdressed—in a tightly tailored black overcoat with velvet collar, homburg hat and cigar in his big teeth. He glanced alertly up and down the street, but did not see us. A white girl was with him—a pretty, delicate little creature, but rather disheveled and forlorn, I thought.

"Who is it?"I asked, when they had gone. The old policeman said solemnly: "That, son, was Eddie Manning—called Eddie the Villain. And take my advice, son, if it means pinching that fellow, never go alone. If you get an urge to talk to him, don't. If he wants to give you a cigarette, refuse it. Never take a drink from him, never go to his place if you want information. Scrub him out of your life—he's the worst man in London."

I was only a beginner in the Metropolitan Police, and did not wish to seem to be teaching my elders and betters their business, but this did seem to be a very negative approach to crime, for a police officer.

"Surely," I said, "he wants dealing with?"

My companion nodded. "He surely does," he said, "but as I've only got a few months to do for my twenty-five years and my pension, I'll leave that to you!"

As I was thinking this one over, he added: "Now remember what I told you, son, and try nothing rash with that fellow. He'll try to dope you, bribe you, trap you. I know two decent youngsters who fell foul of him, and they both simply disappeared. Some well-known men and women have died at his place under drugs or some other diabolical practice."

I did a great deal more thinking about Eddie the Villain in the next couple of years, and discovered a few things about him, although I did not go out of my way either to avoid him or to get in his path. I did not want to make the mistake of taking on a full-scale villain like Eddie Manning before I knew a great deal more about the rules of the game we were both playing on opposite sides. I found that he was from Jamaica and had been in England about ten years, working quite honestly at first in a munitions factory, and then taking a job as jazz drummer with a travelling dance-band. It was here, presumably, that he picked up the threads of drug-trafficking, and was to discover that he had a diabolical genius for it.

He had an elaborately furnished flat in Lisle Street, that was frequented by white girls who seemed willing to do anything for him and his friends, but that was nothing the police could put a finger on, although we strongly suspected that Eddie was giving dope-parties in various parts of London, and injections of cocaine at 10s. per time, also gaming parties with fixed cards and roulette wheels that were fitted with electrically operated brake-shoes, to stop on any number or color that best favored the bank. It was not my job in those days to catch him, and in any case he was a difficult one to get red-handed. He had his own team of strong-arm villains—both white and colored boys who were usually full of drugs, and kept a profitable sideline in protecting prostitutes. Eddie was undoubtedly a villain!

Then I picked up the rumor that—as with so many of his kind—he was beginning to fancy himself too much, and had become careless. I passed on this hint to the proper quarters— I was still in uniform—and the next thing was that detectives arrested Eddie and found opium, an opium pipe and capsules of cocaine, in his possession. In the court it was also stated that a man had died at Eddie's flat from an overdose of heroin, believed to have been supplied by Manning; also a young girl had died from cocaine poisoning, and had neither admitted nor denied that the drug was obtained from Manning.

He received three years' penal servitude, and that took a good deal of the shine out of him. When he came out he opened a little club, and by this time I was a fully experienced detective officer, and he had no terrors for me. I used to call around at his premises regularly to administer a little frightening powder, as we call it. He never fancied me, and would always roll his big white eyeballs sulkily whenever he saw me coming down the steps of his cellar club. I am glad to say that it was as a direct result of information that I picked up and

passed on to my immediate superiors that Eddie got his final
prison sentence, in 1929. I had heard the whisper that he had
gone into the business of receiving stolen property, after he
had been chased out of the drug racket. It was something of a
come-down for his type, but, when the moment was right, I
dropped my whisper and Eddie's abode was raided. It was
found to contain luggage worth £400 that had been stolen
from the then Mr. Duff Cooper and further stolen property
worth over £1,500.

This flat was in St. Ann's Court, Wardour Street, and when
he went to prison that finished his nasty little cellar club in
Berwick Street, which was always filled with prostitutes and
colored boys. Manning's first prison sentence, by the way, was
sixteen months for shooting a man in the street, in Cambridge
Circus!

Unfortunately the end of Eddie Manning did not put an
effective finish to the drug traffic in London. It has, with the
passing of years, veered considerably from cocaine and opium
to marijuana cigarettes, and to the use of such drugs as pethedine and morphine. But it still goes on, and the victims are—as
always—found to be most numerous among the ranks of jazz-
crazy youngsters. There is, I believe, some scientific foundation for the claim that marijuana addiction can help a musician, for this drug has some effect upon that part of the brain
which responds to rhythmical vibrations, and it is a result of
this that the cult of "reefer" smoking has been so closely bound
up with jive musicians and colored men. It is easy enough to
grow—there was a time when drug traffickers were discovered
to be growing marijuana upon desolate bomb-sites around
Liverpool. It is the chopped leaves and seeds of the hemp plant
(*Cannibis indica*) and it will grow anywhere that a dandelion
or nettle will grow. You can find it in canary seed.

It is, however, a great compliment to the fine police work
of Britain that it is such a rarity to find the reefer plant being
cultivated here. The drug traffickers find it more practical to

smuggle it in from the African coastal ports, or from the West Indies, often by way of the oil tankers.

Britain, by the way, has a better record in the battle against dope than any other country in the world. We have nothing to be sensationally alarmed about in this country, but there is no denying that it does go on to a very undesirable extent. I had it brought home to me dramatically the other day, when I took a taxi and found it belonged to one of my friends. Jim the taxi-driver plies around Soho and Leicester Square, and we are frequently meeting each other on our various rounds. He knows London fully as well as I do. And he thinks he knows all the answers. But there is one answer, I found, that old Jim doesn't know. It is the problem of his own daughter, Shirley.

As I paid him, I asked: "How's that pretty daughter of yours, Jim? You didn't show me her photo this trip."

He went suddenly white. "Shirley's O.K.," he said hesitantly, then—"Mr. Fabian, could I ask you some advice?" He put his crumpled glove on the meter-flag, and followed me into a café.

As we stirred coffee, Jim told me about nineteen-year-old Shirley. She was a drug addict.

"We didn't suspect at first, Mr. Fabian. All I knew was that as soon as I got home for my tea, we'd have a blazing row. Usually about her stopping out late. She'd rush up to her poky little bedroom and stay there, sulking. Wouldn't come out. Her mum and me tried to listen to the radio, but we knew what we were really listening for—the sound of our Shirley sneaking downstairs, and the click of the front-door latch as she went out!"

The match-flame he was sucking into his pipe, trembled. "I've never yet struck her," he said. "But no daughter of mine is going to stop out until dawn—hanging around these filthy cafés and dance halls . . . or worse places, for all I know!"

"What can I do, Mr. Fabian? Is it too late to help her?"

There was nothing Jim could do. In my twenty-eight years among London's night life, I have known many drug addicts. Few have ever been cured.

When Shirley stepped, shivering with cold and nerves, into London's night streets, it was not to seek pleasure. She needed drugs. Whatever the price, it had to be paid. Wherever the drug-peddler sold his stuff, she had to go. She couldn't bargain. He had only to sit there, smiling, and wait. . . .

There are far too many girls like her in London's night life today. Spotted at a dance by some schemer who covets her fresh youthfulness, tempted with a habit-forming drug—as a cigarette—candy—a fruit drink—a pinch of snuff "to pep you up!" Within a few months, she cannot remain in her respectable home. She must follow her evil supplier into his underworld. They are truly the damned souls of London. And nearly all of them are under twenty-one!

Chelsea, in the districts around the King's Road and Church Street, is London's headquarters of the cocaine, morphine, pethedine addicts.

Chelsea drug addicts! You wouldn't think them glamorous if you could see them, as I have. That pale, dull young man in frayed grey suit and duffle-coat, who is not enjoying his beer. The middle-aged woman, with dyed hair streaky with grey. She wears black corduroy trousers and a purple utility box-jacket. Her drink, too, is beer. It stays almost untasted.

They don't come to enjoy a drink, nor each other's company. They gather to listen greedily for the whisper of a fellow addict—"I've found a new doctor who . . ." There are ninety-two doctors who are known drug addicts. Five of them are women.

Yes, those are the Chelsea drug addicts. No sparkling artists who loll on silken couches and dream beautifully of paradise. All the Chelsea addicts I know are pale, drawn, indifferent. Usually they have dandruff and watering eyes. Cocaine, morphine, pethedine, are hard to get. Their lives are not much fun. But let them get a youngster in their clutches, and they will poison him—or her—without a qualm. It makes them feel less lonely and doomed.

They are the forlorn remnants of those Bright Young Things—remember them?—who filled the newspapers of twenty-five years ago. Pink champagne, it was in those days, and caffeine pills and glucose injections, to give "pep"—and then . . . cocaine. Today, in London, only these few shivering drug addicts remain, as the ghosts of Mayfair's gay yesterday.

I have tried cocaine. It was given me by a man who would have liked nothing better than to get the Chief of the Flying Squad in his power as a dope addict.

I had a slight cold. "Here, try this, Bob," he said. "It's a new menthol snuff—clears your head wonderfully."

I took a pinch on my thumbnail, and sniffed. There was a sudden freezing sensation in my nose. My face went numb. Then I found myself laughing too loudly, talking too much. . . . I had enough sense to go home.

Next morning was one of shivering nausea and acute misery of mind. I lay and dreamed about that glittering white powder. I wanted it like a thirsty man wants water, like a drowning man wants a gasp of air.

I did not often carry a grudge in my police work. But within a week I had him in jail, where he could not supply anybody—even me—with the stuff.

Most of London's black-market drugs—heroine, cocaine, morphine, pethedine—come these days from stolen medical supplies, forged prescriptions. The drugs that the smugglers concentrate upon are opium and marijuana. In five years, the number of prosecutions for marijuana has increased by 2,100 per cent!

Marijuana is easier to get than morphine. The dried leaf can be sold to drug-peddlers for £50 a pound. You don't need to smoke it. It can be made into candy, chewed like gum, mixed with canned fruit-juice for drinking. The effect is the same. There is not much taste. That's why youth is so vulnerable to it. They don't even need to know they're having it!

Jive musicians still use it persistently. From marijuana addicts, come the bobby-sox terms, like: "It sends me . . . in the groove . . . hep (those in the know) . . . squares (not in the know) . . . out of this world . . . higher than a kite . . ."

Where jive is, youth is. And there, too, is marijuana. It is the drug of America, just as opium is the drug of China. And today, along the Charing Cross Road, where America is worshiped, marijuana claims its victims. Young gangsters use it to get courage. Girls are betrayed by it. It is the easiest, newest weapon of the West End ponce.

Every pound of marijuana can make 1,000 cigarettes. They sell for 7s. 6d. each. . . . Once you are an addict, the drug-peddler may want payment more precious than three half-crowns.

When police raided a private dance hall, The Club Eleven, on April 15, last year, they found Shirley among 250 persons, aged between seventeen and thirty. All were searched. Ten white boys and one negro had packets of marijuana and cocaine. Three were American sailors.

Flung on the dance-hall floor when the raid began, were twenty-three packets of marijuana, handfuls of marijuana cigarettes, a packet of cocaine, a small, sticky wad of prepared opium, and an empty morphine ampoule.

Shirley, giggling stupidly, did not seem to be aware that her ear-lobe was dented by human teeth-marks, and running with blood. She was bandaged, taken home in a police car. It was two a.m. Next day, Shirley wept and made many promises. . . .

Ten weeks later, when the Paramount Dance Hall in the Tottenham Court Road was raided, Shirley was again discovered. This time with colored men. Eight men were arrested —one so drug-crazed that he attacked the police. The marijuana smoker gets mad criminal courage. Give him a gun, and he will shoot.

Shirley did not, this time, give her parents' address. She didn't live there, now. She was living with a swarthy taciturn man of bad breath and worse record. She was chained to him, tighter than ever was medieval slave-girl, by bangles of the dope hunger. It was her nineteenth birthday that week.

Both Club Eleven and Paramount Dance Hall have been closed by the police. But, a few months ago, when twenty-five police officers raided the A to Z Dance Club in Gerrard Street, Shirley was there again!

Blame Shirley? Well, let's go to the case of a wealthy young London medical student whom I arrested for obtaining drugs by forgery. He promised to take a cure, and went to an expensive private sanatorium. Gently, he was "tapered off" from the drug habit. His daily doses grew less. This was his case record:

3rd day: Patient restless, cannot sleep, vomits at food. Complains of cold, although given six blankets.
4th day: Eyes, nose, mouth, watering ceaselessly. Complains of pains. Given sedative but cannot endure contact with bed. Tried to sleep on floor, and received severe abrasions on knees and elbows, from writhing during night.
6th day: Still vomits at sight of food. Alternately sweating, then clammy. Vomiting and diarrhoea. Rising blood pressure, dilated pupils. Yawns and sneezes constantly.
8th day: Complains of aching muscles, burning stomach, severe headache, says "eyeballs hurt as if about to burst". . . .

This patient stayed six months at the sanatorium. He was employed in the open air, given good food, cigarettes, sedatives. Three months after his discharge, he was again in the hands of the police—for stealing drugs from a doctor's car. What chance do you think a young girl has against a habit that grips you like that?

If you smoke heavily, drink regularly, "can't face the day without a cup of tea"—be glad nobody gave you a marijuana cigarette or pinch of cocaine to sniff when you were in your foolish, adventurous 'teens. You possess exactly the same weaknesses as any drug addict.

The hell of dope addicts is that, to get their supplies, they *must* go to the underworld. A boy must steal—a girl must learn to pay in sickening ways—for the handful of dried leaves, the pinch of white numbing powder, the chunk of deadly brown gum, without which their bodies writhe and brains bleed.

A sensitive, cultured negro, who had failed his exams due to marijuana addiction, and landed in Wormwood Scrubs for theft, told me: "I smoke marijuana because it makes me feel less black."

With that, one can sympathize. But Shirley had started using drugs "because it helped me jive better." Poor Shirley!

SHE WAS A VERY RESPECTABLE GIRL, AND she stood trembling with fear and shock, trying to hold her torn frock together decently, until a police car arrived.

The man who had attacked her was trembling, too, with just as much genuine shock as the girl. I held his jacket-sleeve, but he made no effort to tug himself free. I shall not forget the look in his eyes—he looked like a child whose mother had suddenly hit him in the face with his Christmas stocking.

"I don't know what came over me," he kept saying dazedly. "I don't know whatever possessed me."

I had been walking over Mitcham Common, after visiting a friend's house. It was a clear, warm summer evening, with the Sunday Church bells faintly audible upon the wind. I suppose the habit of "giving my eyes a chance" was too strongly a part of my nature for it ever to relax completely, as I walked and enjoyed my pipe, coming as near as a thoroughly trained policeman ever can to minding his own business. I saw this fellow get up from a bench seat and—after an instant's hesitation—begin to follow a girl in light-yellow summery dress, its gay hem swirling modestly but attractively around her knees as she tripped along upon some sensible, preoccupied errand of her own.

It was obvious that the man did not know the girl, and just as plain that she was not in the least interested in attracting his attentions.

This man who had begun to follow her was a respectable-looking citizen, in neat Sunday clothes, stiff white collar and polished shoes, wearing no hat. His hair was greying brown, and the shape of his skull, I noticed, was what in police descriptions we call "an egg-head"—a cranium shaped up to a blunted pyramid. He had a quick glance around and apparently failed to see me because there is always a cone of non-observation, "a blind spot," behind a man who tries to look behind when he is hurrying forward, and I happened to be in it. It was not skill on my part, but it just happened to be that way. Looking back upon the incident, I felt it was unfortunate that he did not see me, for if he had he would never have attacked the girl.

I could see the path she was taking, across the open Common, and realized that if I hurried in a somewhat transverse direction, I could probably reach the distant clump of bushes without attracting too much attention to myself. There seemed to be nobody else about.

I was a little too late, as it happened, for the man reached her and hit at her several times. They were unskilled blows and it was only because she was a slender little creature that she succumbed to them, but she fell down and he pounced upon her, with no more hesitation than a cat upon a beetle, and began to rip at her clothing.

I shouted, to stop him doing any serious damage, and caught him after a brief chase, for he was not in very good running condition. I brought him back to the girl, and we all three walked to the nearest telephone-box.

When the report of the subsequent court case was printed in the newspapers it sounded like a dastardly attack, and you might have thought the man was Jack-the-Ripper in person. He wasn't. He was a bewildered little chap who looked as dazed and surprised at himself for what he had done, as if somebody had hypnotized him. It was his first offense, and he was a respectably married man with two children almost grown up. His wife stood by him, and that was, to my mind, the most pitiable part of the entire affair.

Now, why do these things happen? Had that man any real hopes of being able to commit rape on Mitcham Common and get away with it? Did he even stop to think about his chances? I am sure that he would have given twenty times more careful consideration to buying himself a seven-and-sixpenny tie, than he did to performing an act that cost him his reputation and freedom, his respectable job and hopes of security in old age, and blasted the happiness of his wife and children. His boy, I remember, had to leave Grammar School because he couldn't face it after what his father had done.

The things that go on inside the human brain are a study for the trained psychologist. But the police officer must not ignore them, for the key to many a strange and otherwise inexplicable crime lies often in the subconscious mind of the guilty person, in that mysterious box where he or she tries to keep the lid shut down on the primitive sex instinct.

It may surprise many people to know that at the various Police Colleges in Britain, and particularly at Hendon where the Metropolitan officers are taught the deeper intricacies of their calling, they have lectures and discussions upon sex that would not disgrace an international convention of university lecturers. It is fully realized that the job of the London police-man is complicated by a need to have an almost clinical knowledge of the minds of those who offend against sexual morality, for I think it is true that a person who is ready to transgress against the moral code is already a member of the underworld, though he may himself not be aware of it, and though his conduct sheet is as yet without any blemish.

The policeman today pays very careful heed to these things, and has done for many years past. His job is made more difficult by the fact that the law is still considerably behind the times in its approach to sexual morality. It is not the police who are behind the times, I repeat, but the law itself. And the remedy lies, not with the police, but with the citizen, to get this cleared up. For the law is never a dreary, dead thing. It is not musty books in lawyers' offices. The law is a living, stirring plasma that grows upon the face of civilization, and is constantly changing with it. The law is the conscience and voice of the ordinary citizen, and the lawyer—the judge—the politician—are forever running a step behind the citizen, carrying forward the living skeins of the law, to link them up as quickly as they possibly can with the need of the times.

That may sound like rather heavy going, and I do not mind admitting that it is based on a paper I once wrote for a promotion examination.

It is not the job of the policeman to criticize the law. Like the policeman in *Les Miserables*—"my job is to enforce the Law—good, bad or indifferent—but the Law to the letter!" And when a well-respected citizen suddenly takes off his trousers and dashes down the main shopping street, it is not the task of the police officer to consider whether the man is mentally sick, whether he has ever done this sort of thing before, or is ever likely to do it again. It is his job to arrest him. Every argument that might be pleaded on behalf of the trouserless one can also be pleaded for the murderer. Nine times out of ten he may never do it again. In the eyes of the police, once is enough!

It is the task of the police to protect the normal citizen against the abnormal citizen, and not to pry too deeply into

the various conditions of sexual repression that either might
be suffering.

But I think the task of the police would be made simpler
if the law would get itself immediately up to date on certain
questions. I think everybody—certainly every police officer—
has heard of Professor Freud, who more than sixty years ago
began to publish the results of his researches, and it is upon
these that—whatever we may think of Freud's theories—nearly
all our modern theory of sex is built. Yet in this time the law
has scarcely changed at all. It would be almost a parallel if
the law of Britain did not yet acknowledge the existence of
electricity and aviation, or recognized their effects upon the
lives of people and crime.

I remember a lecture at Police College by a very distinguished psychologist and author—it was Mr. Nigel Balchin—
and I think that an extract from it may be of general interest
as indicating the level upon which police officers discuss and
study these matters:

> "The law (today) has its origins in the medieval system
> by which offenses against sexual morality were dealt with
> by the Ecclesiastical Courts.
>
> "The Church had its own code of purely *religious* law
> under which, quite apart from an offense against society or
> another citizen, a man could offend against God, and be
> punished for it. With the disappearance of the Ecclesiastical
> Courts, there was no power to impose what was presumed
> to be God's will, or to punish people for disobeying it. The
> function was therefore assumed by the Civil Courts, and it
> is the vestiges of this function—the enforcement of religious
> rule—that we see in much of today's law relating to sex.
> When one of you gentlemen has to enforce some law about
> not playing this or that on Sunday, you are not enforcing a
> democratic law supported by the mass of citizens, and you
> are not protecting them against anything but themselves.

You are simply fulfilling one of the old functions of the
Ecclesiastical Courts, who were prepared to lay down,
and enforce, regulations about God's views and intentions
on any subject under the sun.

"The Church in those times had a great belief in the
basic depravity of human beings. It believed that man was
born bad, and that there was a constant battle for his soul
between Christianity on one side and the devil on the
other. In this battle, the man himself was free to choose
his side, and to become good or bad as the case might be.
The sinner and the criminal, therefore, were those who had
deliberately chosen to range themselves against Church and
State—who had declared war on the law, and were to be
treated accordingly.

"Underlying this was a belief that it was not only possible for all men to be good and moral citizens, but *equally*
possible for them to be so. And this remains the principle
of law to this day. The law recognizes the existence of
insanity—a state in which a man is not aware of the nature
of his actions. But short of insanity, it assumes that all men
are normal, fully and equally responsible for their actions
and in so far as they act abnormally and illegally, that they
do so deliberately and of malice."

I remember once reading about a Chinese emperor who
decided that it would be much neater if everybody was the
same size—particularly with the soldiers of his armies. He had
a measuring rod made to the height of what he thought the
ideal soldier should be. Every soldier who was too tall had a
portion hacked from his legs, and any luckless warrior who
was too short was stretched out to the required length.

This really occurred in history. To us it seems bizarre and
comical. Sometimes one wonders if future generations will not
find our own approach to sex and crime as pathetically imprac-
tical?

If families are crowded together in slum tenements, so that

they all sleep sprawled over one mattress in the corner of the room—as was common enough in London when I was a young constable, and still exists today—the chances of the abominable crime of incest being committed are a great deal stronger than in a comfortable suburban house such as you probably live in, where the 'teen-age son might hammer impatiently upon the bathroom door when his sister is in too long washing her hair, but would in no circumstances intrude upon her.

It is not only in the slums that the seeds of warped minds are laid. The way a child is brought up, the way its parents talk and behave, whether or not they go to church—all have a big effect on what sort of citizen an individual is going to become.

Even the amount of sex a person might have within himself varies tremendously. The one thing we can be sure of is that everybody has it in some degree—this instinct to continue the species. It is like the instinct to struggle against drowning, or to wince away from a flame.

The law of the country permits a boy or girl to marry at the age of sixteen—they are legally entitled to marry before they are legally permitted to vote! And physically they are fully equipped for marriage, just as the law recognizes that a boy of fourteen years old is physically capable of committing rape.

But the actual fact is that a good citizen cannot start marrying at the age of sixteen. He—and she—must wait usually for about ten years before arriving at a sensible state for taking the responsibility of marriage. Then, when they are married, the law requires that they must have no sexual experience other than with their married partner.

I do not see how you could change the law on this. I just do not see how you could. As long as marriage exists, the law has to be like that. And today we teach sex in schools. We instruct—as it were—a child in how to drive a motor-car and then leave him alone with his fascinating toy after telling him that he may not drive until he is married! We expect a great deal of self-restraint to be shown by our citizens, and I think we are entitled to expect it. We are not animals, and it is a long time in history since we dwelt and thought as animals.

Inevitably, the average citizen—in order to be a good citizen —*must* keep himself under control. He may want £100, but he is not allowed to steal it. He may want to have a girl before marriage, but he is wrong to give way to this temptation.

So, from schooldays onwards, the good citizen must learn to thrust all his primitive sex instincts in a box and sit on the lid. There was a time when we all believed in hell and eternal punishment, and every child was taught that God watched him in each deed and thought. That must have been a great help in resisting temptation. It was like putting a safety strap around the box. It is a pity that so many of us do not have this belief today.

Some psychologists say that it is wrong to keep this pressure in what they call our subconscious minds. They think it should be released—that we should be allowed to "let off steam." As a policeman, as a father, and as a respectable citizen, I cannot agree with this. We can't all go letting off steam. We *must* learn to sit on the lid. We have set for ourselves a standard of behavior that is better than the animals, and we have got to keep to it even if some of us get hurt in the process—just as in a war.

It is undeniable that the thickness of the box-lid, as well as the amount of pressure from inside, varies so much with each individual that we may pity—even though we have to punish —the person who explodes, like the egg-headed man on Mitcham Common. I would not have remitted one day of his sentence. The knowledge that he was bitterly punished makes it easier for me, and for millions like me, to remain good citizens. But I pity him, just as I would pity a man born blind.

There are some maiden ladies who have never had a real love affair, but who burn up their repressed sexual energy doing good work—social work in the slums, or in hospitals. They might well be horrified to think that their undoubted goodness was merely the charcoal of burned-up sexual energy.

But although it probably is—and I concede that much to the psychologist—the work they have done is still good work, necessary, and helpful to us all, and a damned sight more constructive to the hopes of civilization than raping girls on Mitcham Common.

There are others who are not so fortunate in being able to divert this repressed sexual energy into decent channels. These types of people explode. Nearly always they have been thoroughly respectable until the instant of the explosion. My police experience has shown me that they are as bewildered as could be, when they realize what they have done. They have sat on the box as hard as they knew how, but it has gone BOOM! underneath them, and I think that in a few more years, when our psychologists are no longer groping like men striking matches in a dark cavern, but have reached a condition where they know what they are doing, and have more competently explored the dark ravines of the human brain, the law will be changed to give more mercy to such people. But not yet—not yet, unless you want to destroy the incentive that every well-behaved citizen has for retaining his self-control.

I think better of my fellow-man than to say that he is good only because he fears punishment, although I would be denying all my years of practical police experience—all that I have seen and known—if I were to say that the fear of being found out is not a powerful deterrent against committing crime.

But I do say that a child is taught to be a good child, and later to become a good citizen, because he is brought up in the belief that goodness is expected of him, and that the friendship and regard of his fellows will be at once withdrawn from him if he ceases to control himself. The punishment of prison is not simply in locking him away and forcing him to keep to a cheerless routine. That happens to monks, and they find joy in it. The punishment of prison is in the disgrace, and if we rob prison of its disgrace, and release criminals from the fear of the results of being found out in their crimes, then we will be letting hell loose upon earth.

SOME MEN THINK IT CLEVER TO HAVE THE names and telephone numbers of a few immoral women in their personal memo-books. Frequently, when such men have had a drink or two, they produce these books in bars and boast about them.

I can see nothing to boast about in knowing prostitutes. When I was Chief of London's Vice Squad I had the names in my office ledger of every known prostitute in London . . . their phoney names and genuine names, ages, photos, descriptions, habits, weaknesses, regular cronies and haunts—and even the names of their sorrowing, respectable relatives (this last for the purpose of identifying any of our Jezebels if, and when, she was fished up from the stinking mud of London River). We did a fairly sound job of checking upon the movements of the "regulars," and noted when they left Town for a week end or a brief holiday abroad. This we did in case they never came back. Being murdered is one of the risks that a prostitute takes in her trade.

There were thousands of girls' names upon my books—not one of them had any more morals than a hen. What makes a girl become a prostitute? I think I can tell you—it is sheer laziness, and vanity. Added to this, one may perhaps take into account the clinical fact that nearly every successful prostitute is sexually frigid. Her love-gestures are as automatic and insincere as the wide smile on the face of a tired chorus-girl.

A whore is a bad apple. There is a big brown bruise on her soul, of self-indulgence and selfishness. I do not think that there exists in London any such person as an honest prostitute. They taint any flesh they touch.

Men are almost incredibly fatuous in their approach to a prostitute. It is small wonder that they are so easily made fools of by these women, whose name for their customers—for every client they have ever had or ever hope to have—is "The Mug." They never consider him as anything else but a fool. And for once they are right. Sometimes they call him, in thieves' vernacular, "The Steamer," which is rhyming slang that derives from "steam-tug" and still signifies "Mug."

The great majority of Mugs are soft-hearted men. Nine out of ten of these men are looking for romance. They have a few drinks, and wander out into the streets, hoping to discover under some lamp-post a young creature who has been driven by hunger or despair into proffering her body. The Mug is convinced within himself that the girl will look upon it as a very lucky evening when he found her, because he is so much better than her usual type of customer.

He isn't. He is just the same. He is a Mug, like all the rest. Even his conversation is the same. "How did a nice girl like you get into this kind of life?" She smiles and gives him the stock answer, as she has probably done twice already that evening.

He visualizes a situation in which he and the girl will go and have a romantic drink together, and then to her room, where he will make love to her and give her a little money, and she will remember him always as the one outstanding moment of her otherwise drab, sordid existence. . . .

The prostitutes can spot the Mug coming. They can pick him out by his way of walking, by the manner in which he carries his head and moves his eyes. They do not see him as the romantic character he imagines himself to be, and even though he is a six-footer in Service uniform, with a chest full of medals, he is still just another Mug to them.

The girls start the evening well spaced out along the recognized trade-routes—the half-lit streets behind Piccadilly or Leicester Square, around the maze of Shepherd's Market, and in the purlieus of Paddington. It is only later on, when they have taken a customer or two, and are becoming careless, or when they have had no luck at all and are becoming sulky, that they congregate in twos and threes for a triumphant or embittered gossip. They are as hard as nails. The romantic, half-drunken Mug has almost exactly as much chance of actually discovering a spark of romance upon a street corner, as of picking up a well-filled wallet in the gutter. There are several sound, practical reasons why his chances are negligible.

Firstly, there are at least two highly experienced organizations that constantly scour and survey the streets and cafés of London, night and day, looking for any girl who appears to be uncertain of her future.

The first of these organizations is the Metropolitan Police. It is particularly the duty of the Women Police to patrol around the railway stations, the long-distance bus terminals, the all-night cafés, milk bars, public parks and the prostitute-ridden districts of the West End and W.2, seeking just such inexperienced girls as the Mug hopes to find. Night after night —every night—a big blue police tender, known colloquially as "The Children's Wagon," waits outside each of the bigger public parks.

And every night it collects its quota of young girls who have escaped from remand homes, detention institutions, or who answer to the descriptions that are circulated through London from every police force in the country, of girls missing from home for various reasons.

Every policeman on his beat knows, by sight and name, the habitual prostitutes. If he sees a new face he will stop and talk to her—ask where she is from, what is her name, and so on. There are a dozen charges he can pick her up on, none of them important, but enough to get her into the police station, where relatives or other responsible authorities can be contacted. He will do this without hesitation when he sees a girl soliciting, who appears to have any shreds of innocence left upon her soul. That is normal routine. And it is a very tightly knotted network indeed. A girl walking slowly, alone, through London, even in the daytime, attracts immediate attention. After dark, she becomes increasingly conspicuous.

Another organization which carries out a similar unceasing search is that of the underworld itself. Many men in London live upon the immoral earnings of prostitutes. The name for such men is "Ponces" or "Johnsons," and they are the lowest form of animal life on the criminal scale, although you might not think so to look at them, for they can—when business is good—dress quite expensively and are often surly, determined-looking types, apparently well able to look after themselves in a fight. Yet any pickpocket or screwsman despises them, and will "shop" them to the law as soon as not. These ponces sometimes drift into their disreputable destiny from respectable lives, and some are Army deserters; but more often they are born into the underworld of London and know its warrens and its devices and its strange language, as a skilled gamekeeper knows the secrets of copse and hedgerow.

These men know where to look for girls "on the run" in London, or for girls who are, for any other reason, desperate and unprotected. They scurry in and out of cheap "kaffs," loaf around likely places, and have a hundred ways of knowing all about girls who are heading for the streets. When a girl escapes from Borstal, or from a remand home, the odds are that she has the address of some Johnson already in her purse, or of some kaff where she will be sure to meet one within five minutes.

The ordinary Mug has not much hope of picking up any doomed innocent upon the streets of London after the police harvesting machine has swept over them, and the sharp-eyed, busybody professional Johnsons have attended with their own diabolical skill to the job of gleaning any stray that might have chanced to miss the official eye.

Finally, there is the preventative of the known prostitutes themselves. A novice girl who walks through—say—Shepherd's Market in search of a man will get a sharply tipped shoe-heel in her face within less time than it takes her to smoke a cigarette, unless her own protection has previously been amply established. By this I mean that she must already be the property of some particular ponce or group of ponces, who will take at least fifty per cent of her earnings, which she will pay to them, by arrangement beforehand, for the right "to work." This goes for the more notorious streets of Piccadilly and Leicester Square, and—indeed—for any place in London where one might ordinarily expect to find prostitutes.

Every prostitute that you may see upon such notorious sites is certainly paying at least £20 per week, and often much more, for the right to be there. She is not likely to stand by and watch a strange girl infringe upon her costly pitch. If she is herself not inclined to take off her shoe and deal with the intruder, helped gladly by any other girl of her trade and acquaintance in the vicinity, she has only to send for her Johnson, who will muss up the newcomer with all the ferocity and lack of hesitation that one can expect from a type whose only pride is in his ability to intimidate a woman. He will shred her face unforgettably. A slender phial of acid dropped inside her clothing and then shattered with a blow from his fist. Or he can set fire to her hair. . . .

The Johnson feels fairly safe in performing these outrages, for they will be done in a quiet corner—after all, the girl's whole

purpose in being there is to take a man into a quiet corner,
isn't it?—and his alibi will be carefully prepared in advance.
Or, if he is reckless enough, he will just do his job of butchery
on the street.

So much, then, for the hopeful Mug's chances of encounter-
ing any kind of romance at the street corner or beneath the
street lamp. What he will encounter will be a very tough,
experienced business woman, as strong as a young bullock,
with legs like marble—she does so much standing about!—and
with the mental attitude of a fairground boxing-booth prize-
fighter. She has it all calculated, viciously and expertly. Somewhere nearby is a hired bedroom—technically known as a
"lumber"—because it is to this room that she "lumbers" her
mugs. You will find precious little signs of femininity or cozi-
ness there. She does not live in her "lumber," but uses it
strictly for business.

Her own flat will be out in the suburbs, as likely as not, or
in another part of the West End. The Mug will never see that.

Why is a "lumber" necessary? Well, there are several
reasons, apart from the simple convenience of having it handy
to her "beat." The rental of the district, and the purchase price
of the necessary tolerance, is very high—the landlord certainly
knows what it is being used for—and almost any little room
will suffice. Also, the comfortlessness of the "lumber" is a
business asset. She will allow perhaps five minutes for preliminaries, for talking with glib friendliness and laughing at
all the Mug's pathetic jokes—which she has probably heard
three or four times that evening already from other Mugs—and
another five or ten minutes to get him to the "lumber," including a couple of minutes for a kiss and a squeeze in the
corridor, perhaps, and a suitable opportunity to demand the
money in advance from him—she will ask for £5 and usually
be content with £3, or £2 as rock-bottom price—and then she
produces the latch-key from its hiding-place, and lets him in.

It will be a sparse room, its only furniture usually quite
cheap although not necessarily nasty—and the only signs of

personal property might be her umbrella and plastic mackintosh for when it rains, some over-shoes, perhaps a depleted gin bottle (never more than two inches of gin in the bottom, for fear the Mug drinks it, and thus sends up the overhead!), and, concealed in a cupboard for her personal use, the apparatus for making a cup of tea. A fat chance Mr. Mug has of being made to feel at home, of being made even to feel wanted. Every instant he spends in the prostitute's "lumber" is time grudged by her. If she can get through her grisly little performance in less than ten minutes, then she will be back on her beat all that much sooner.

So she will remove her shoes and make other essential adjustments of garments as speedily as she possibly can, and wait impatiently for the Mug's advances, and is as likely as not to say: "Come on, can't you hurry it up?" just at what he would have imagined was the tenderest moment. . . .

She will certainly discourage Mr. Mug from anything in the nature of amorous delicacy that might be likely to cause her to reach any climax of satisfaction. It is undeniably true that the greater majority of London's prostitutes are very much undersexed, almost at zero by contrast with an ordinary, respectable housewife, and this is a professional asset to them, for they can approach the whole matter with an air of almost clinical detachment and contempt for the client.

Prostitution in London is big business, and although Mr. Mug's £3 may represent his entire surplus spending money, to the Piccadilly prostitute £3 is calculated as less than half an hour's work—or somewhere between one-fifth and one-tenth of her nightly receipts.

That is the procedure in dealing with the innocent, wide-eyed, "mushy" Mug—the provincial business man in London on an overnight stay, the young men on works outings or university escapade, the visiting rugger club members, the holidaymaker in London, the overseas visitor, or serviceman on leave, the plantation manager on home furlough, the suburban husband who has quarrelled with his wife, or whose wife has gone to visit relatives. These make up probably four-fifths of the London prostitute's regular trade. She rarely sees them again, nor particularly wants to do, and if the Mugs were honest with themselves, the feeling would be entirely mutual . . . though it is surprising what a little retrospective romantic imagination can do, even to such a scrambled, sordid interlude!

If men who have come to London and fallen dupe to a Piccadilly prostitute would only be honest with themselves and with everybody they afterwards talk with about their "adventure," prostitution in London could be diminished by seventy-five per cent almost overnight. It is so villainously sordid, and unsatisfying.

The remaining twenty per cent of men who keep the business alive with their patronage are not describable as "innocents" in any way. These are the regulars—the clients whose perverted morality fully matches that of their paid hostesses.

These "regular" clients are all potentially criminal men. It may surprise some of them to be told that they are quite as well known to the police as the women they hire, although they have not necessarily got any criminal record!

Something is wrong inside their brains. They are "queer men"—fetishists—males in whose mentality some wheel has come unshafted. There is one of them, a mild, elderly little chap, who holds a respected position with a London insurance company and is known to every prostitute in London, I should think, as "Mary."

This pitiful imbecile comes regularly to the West End, carrying a neat, brown attaché case in which he has a housemaid's frilled cap and apron, a dustpan and handbrush. He pays £5 without demur to any prostitute who will take him to her room, where he puts the maid's cap on his ridiculous half-bald head, ties the apron around his waist (he does not even remove his jacket) and kneels down with his dustpan and brush, scuffing energetically at the carpet at her feet. All that she has to do is to repeat some such rubbish as: "Faster, Mary —you must work more quickly!" and after about ten minutes of this degrading pantomime, if the girl can keep her face straight, that is all there is to it.

What goes on in the mind of such a man, I am too much of a policeman and too little of a psychiatrist, to say. He knows that he is an object of ridicule and contempt, but persists with his behavior, as far as I know, although it is fortunately no longer a part of my business to be daily informed upon the activities of such strange denizens of the twilight world between sanity and dementia.

It is vitally necessary for a successful policeman in London to be well informed upon such activities, for perverts are always teetering upon the brink of serious crime, and one can never be sure when they will not spill over into it. When Neville Heath, posing as an Army colonel on leave and with rows of false decorations, picked up Marjorie Gardner at the bar of the Panama Club he wanted her in order to tie her hands and feet and beat her. Handsome as he was, and a splendid figure of a man, he was in his own way just as lamentably inadequate and perverted as the little man known as "Mary." There can be no doubt, I think, that Neville Heath did not intend to murder Marjorie Gardner in the outset, but merely to practice his peculiar obsessions. And it was also known to police observers of the West End scene that Marjorie Gardner was by no means unacquainted with such brutal and humiliating activities.

Something went amiss, and Heath carried his indulgences too far. Marjorie Gardner died of hemorrhage, stabbed internally by the haft of a hunting whip, and the only thing that Heath could think to do, apparently, in the few days of freedom left to him as a hunted man, was to repeat the style of murder upon another girl—this time a clearly innocent victim —presumably in the hope of showing himself to be insane. He began as a mere pervert, and he ended on the scaffold as a murderer. The police, as representatives of the will of society, could not in this case put him in court earlier upon charges of perversion, but only, eventually, upon charges of murder after two girls had died.

And, similarly, when two men with distorted minds become physically attracted to each other, they do not necessarily commit any offence against the person—that is to say, neither man trespasses upon the privacy or rights of the other, nor performs any act that is against the other man's will—but the almost inevitable outcome, as with the Neville Heaths of London, is that both men will sooner or later commit a mutual offence against the public moral code. And that is an offence, just as much as indecent exposure, even if it is performed in private. The law has been described as "an Ass," but the law is not such an ass as to close her eyes to the fact that you can shock and injure a respectable citizen without necessarily coming into physical contact with him. If you shake your fist in a man's face, you commit assault; if you drop a bus-ticket upon the pavement, you commit disorderly conduct. Similarly, if your behavior is so outrageous as to become offensive to normal citizens, then you have committed an offence. Therefore, we of the police must keep our eyes upon these sad, bewildering and despicable people, even though their wrongful acts are committed behind locked doors.

The administration of the law in England is not as straightforward as I think it should be. Frequently I have heard complaints from decent people who have been shocked by the sight of the prostitutes of London. "Why," they ask, "do the police not prevent them?"

The simple answer is that if the citizen would give the police the powers, they would prevent it all right. But the police possess no such authority. They have to proceed against this eyesore and this moral menace as foxily as an Oriental horse-dealer. Did you, the honest citizen, know that you have withheld from your police force any lawful right to arrest a prostitute as such?

It cannot be done. A police officer may know perfectly well

that a girl who is parading shamelessly up and down Piccadilly is a prostitute, but he must wait until she "solicits to the
annoyance of passers-by." In fact, she is never arrested for
actual prostitution, nor for soliciting, but only for behaving in
such a way that she has made a man step off the pavement to
avoid her, or has grasped his arm, or has halted him in his free
and lawful passage along the street.

That is why the fine inflicted next day is always so ridi-
culously small. She is being fined for obstruction, just as a
motorist, or a barrow-boy, or a pavement artist, might be fined,
or a shopkeeper with his window-blind too low.

So she pays her £2 and considers it merely a part of her
normal business overhead, just as the rent of her "lumber" is,
or the cost of her lipstick, or the heavy percentage she pays for
her underworld "protection."

The only real damage that a police officer can inflict upon
her, is to arrest her early in the evening, before she has had
time to collect her quota of clients. And the punishment thus
inflicted is not the trivial amount of the fine, but the loss of her
expected fees. Can you imagine the heavy temptation that you,
the citizen whose vote and whose publicly voiced wishes
formulate the law of the land, are imposing upon police officers whose pay is not lavish, when it becomes easily worth a
prostitute's while to offer him two or three pounds—not to
refrain from arresting her—but merely to defer his arrest of
her until later in the evening? I think it is one of the lesser-
recognized miracles of London that so few Metropolitan constables accept these bribes, when by doing so they could easily
double or treble their salaries.

I KNOW A WOMAN WHO LIVES IN A MEWS flat that is so near to Piccadilly Circus, if you were to throw a stone from Eros Statue, you could hit her windows.

She makes far more money than does the Commissioner of Scotland Yard and pays no income tax upon any of it. She is probably among the half-dozen richest women in London today, if one judges by income. Certainly she is among the most vicious and depraved.

I have heard her called "Dominating Catherine," and sometimes "Red Katy," and she possesses in full measure that valuable attribute of the successful prostitute—an unloving coldness for all men. Katy hates men, despises them and treats them with unconcealed contempt. They pay her hundreds of pounds a week, to the accompaniment of a stream of vituperation and abuse from her, and they like it!

Her trade begins at her very front door, which is shamelessly unusual. This door is distinguished by an awning, and the doorway itself is covered with a crimson plush curtain. There is a huge bell-push, but the impatient client never gets as far as pushing this bell until he has made an appointment—often days ahead by telephone. He is treated with scorn over the phone, and when finally he is given grudging permission to "come round at three o'clock a week on Wednesday," he is well aware that it will be necessary for him to thrust at this enormous bell-push for several minutes before he wins any attention.

Her clients are all psychotic masochists—men whose perverse, nightmare need is to be humiliated and physically hurt by the object of their lust. And Kate is still a very handsome woman, with hair that once was fiercely red and today is streaked with grey.

She has been plying her trade successfully in London for over fifteen years now. Once she had a husband: nobody knows what happened to him, or what manner of man he was, or why —or indeed, how—she was ever persuaded to marry him. But she has two sons, nearly in full manhood. One is at university, and the other at a very famous school. Kate entered their names for this school on the day after each of them was born! Her clients include many distinguished men, and if one day she were to publish her reminiscences—which I know she never will do, for the sake of her sons—she could cause consternation among the pages of Debrett. I do not know what the doctors think about this subject, but my own experience as Chief of London's Vice Squad has been that you do not find nearly so many masochists among men of humble or peasant origin, as among those who were born into aristocratic, wealthy families.

I believe one possible reason for this may be that this type of masochism too often has its beginnings with sadistic nannies, or school experiences. Most of Kate's clientele are middle-aged.

So there he is, this misguided man, whose family and friends know nothing of his peculiarity, thumping and pounding at Kate's plush-curtained front door, concealed less than two hundred yards from Piccadilly Circus. And the door itself is remarkable. Sharp nails have been hammered through it, points outward, and it would hardly be possible to find space to hammer one additional nail into that door! Her clients find their first pleasure in hurting themselves against its hideous surface.

She opens the door to them, at last, in a storm of abuse for their impatience, of acid scorn for their weakness in coming to her at all, and reviles them for "polluting" her dwelling-place with their presence. Most of this is quite genuine, for Kate really does despise her customers, and it is an essential part of her attractiveness to them that she makes this vigorously clear.

"See," she says, "you filthy, contemptible, ill-mannered pig —how dare you show impatience at my door!"

The mews flat is sumptuously furnished, with great vases and pedestals of flowers. "Wipe your filthy feet!" orders Kate, "take your shoes off—I won't have you dirtying my carpets!"

The client must pass through her bedroom—he is not permitted to linger in it—and goes into the room beyond, which she calls her "operation-room." Nobody has ever been permitted to linger in Kate's private bedroom. I know one client who offered Kate £500 for the "privilege" of lying across her bed while she whipped him—and she refused. "You contemptible beast!" she said, "I would never be able to sleep in my room again, if I had let you so much as touch my bed!"

The "operation-room" is harshly lit. It contains a weird assortment of devices for inflicting pain. All the time, the client is pleading with Kate for her forgiveness, promising he "will be good," while she lays into him with the whiplash of her tongue, and afterwards with her collection of torture-implements.

It is, I suppose, a form of hypnotism, in which the victim willingly acquiesces, the lure and the fascination to him being that he should be treated as if he were a helpless child under the domination of a sadistic adult. The sight of this performance, although entirely pathetic and completely obscene, must also be laughably ridiculous to a healthy mind—but Kate's clients do not possess the blessing of healthy minds. They are obviously men who are mentally ill, and, in some way that is beyond our understanding, this "treatment" gives them relief. They gladly pay her sums of £50-£100 for a "session" that seldom lasts for as much as two hours.

Sometimes a young girl is brought in to do the actual whipping. Kate's is not the only establishment of this kind in London. There are dozens of them. On September 22, 1953, a girl of seventeen gave evidence against a woman who was tried for "influencing her to perform immoral practices," and described how she was taught to employ a whip with leather thongs and a two-foot malacca cane upon "customers" at a flat in Buckingham Palace Road.

But Kate is the incredible doyen of them all. So far she has escaped prosecution. There is a whole showcase in the Hendon Police College Museum of instruments captured in raids upon similar premises in London's West End. These include, not only whips, canes, straps and diabolically vile devices, but even a pair of butter-paddles, such as grocery assistants use.

Red Kate works only five days per week. Her fees—and her weekly receipts—are fully equal to those of the most highly paid Harley Street surgeon. Kate pays no tax on hers. It is all profit.

At week-ends she retires to her pleasant house not far from Sunningdale, and is understood by her distinguished neighbors to be a wealthy widow who has an important post with a Government confidential department! Her work is certainly confidential.

I was discussing this type of woman recently with a business acquaintance in the West End, who asked me: "How do women of that type manage not to pay income tax? Surely, when they become owners of valuable properties, they are finally tracked down by the Inland Revenue, and are required to explain their sources of income?"

I told him that, so far as I knew, it was undoubtedly true that they did receive these revenue inquiries. But, in the case of Red Kate—and in most other instances that I know—the tax official's inquiry is answered with the bland, brazen statement: "I am a prostitute in London!" Thereafter, they hear no more. The Income Tax authorities are understandably reluctant to make demands upon the earnings of prostitutes. In the same way, these women evaded all National Service and billeting responsibilities during the war. Any woman or girl who filled in her calling-up preliminary papers with "Occupation—prostitute" never heard any more from the startled authorities.

From the legal viewpoint, it is not an offence to be a prostitute, but it is an offence to benefit from the immoral earnings of a prostitute. The tax collector is probably well advised to leave them alone, as things are at present!

The real danger of having people like Red Kate active in London is that they pander to perverts, and it is from the ranks of perverts that practically all the most savage, puzzling crimes emerge.

I can tell you a fair amount about perverts: it is the business of every police officer to know them, to recognize them for what they are. The police do not study these people because they find them amusing, but because years of experience have taught how deadly dangerous they can become.

We do not call them by any of the Latin names used by psychologists. We call them perverts and we think of them as perverts, and there are many more of these people in London than ordinary citizens realize!

In fact, I do not think that the average person knows much about perverts at all. I would be only too happy to leave him in that ignorance, if it were blissful: but it is the attitude of the ostrich. Not until the man in the street knows more about perverts will we be able to get proper laws for controlling them. And until the policeman has proper and adequate laws for controlling these people, he must fail in his results, however hard he may strive to do his duty.

The one type of perversion that the law vaguely recognizes is that of homosexuality. This is an offence against decency, and is punishable by heavy imprisonment. As a law-breaking act it is a parallel with robbery with violence. You may walk the streets of London for months and never see an actual instance of robbery with violence. But there is not one night in London when—if you go to the right places—you will fail to see an example of persons soliciting to commit the offence of homosexuality.

The underworld term for these men is "Queers." The puzzling thing is that they are usually normal in appearance and manner. The cheap antics of stage comedians have made most people think of the "pansy" as a lisping, mincing creature who uses perfume and nail varnish. This is not correct. Of all the men I have seen convicted for offences of homosexuality, I would defy anybody to pick nine out of ten of them from any ordinary assembly of men. Quite a number of them are married.

In the underworld of the brain—the twilight world of morals—where perversion has its existence, there is a great deal more going on than simple homosexuality. There are, for instance, men who take an unnatural pleasure in women's hair. They collect photographs of girls with long hair, and go into ecstasies if they can persuade any of their women friends to allow them to brush her hair. That sounds harmless enough, doesn't it? I will tell you then of the case history of a London murderer. He was a hair fetishist. It was a few years ago, now, in the days when most schoolgirls used to wear their hair in long plaits. This man, who was in every appearance normal, and of quite respectable social standing, was traveling one day in a bus and sat behind two schoolgirls whose plaits dangled behind the seat-back. He could not resist touching them. They did not, apparently, notice him. Soon he had developed the daily habit of travelling in the bus that contained a swarm of home-going schoolchildren, and would do his best to find a seat behind girls with plaits. As always with a perversion, the more he indulged it the stronger and more shameless it became. Sometimes his touching of their plaits was noticed, but the worst that ever happened was a sulky or half-timid snatching away of the plait. Most girls with plaits are quite accustomed to having them pulled and handled.

One day he touched the hair of a girl who, becoming aware of what was happening, merely giggled. He followed her off the bus, and was successful in persuading her to allow him to unbraid her hair and replait it. He gave her half a crown for this.

It began to develop in his brain as an obsession that he wanted not merely to touch the hair of these children, but actually to possess their plaits. You will have noticed stories occasionally in the newspapers of men who are arrested for cutting off the plaits of girls. All such offenders are hair-fetishists. And this man was just such another. He did succeed in snipping off one or two such trophies, and hurried down the bus-steps with them, unobserved.

It soon became too risky to continue his activities in the omnibuses. He went into the parks and playgrounds. And there came the inevitable climax of disaster when he had successfully bribed a little girl to permit him to unbraid her hair, and then could not resist cutting off a great quantity of it. She began to cry, and all at once he realized how the story would look in the newspapers, when the inevitable course of complaint—arrest—prosecution—imprisonment had run. He silenced her by killing her. And, when we finally caught him, in his bedroom were eleven plaits of hair, and dozens of little snippets. That is the way of perversion: it begins with a small, half-ashamed indulgence, and grows rapidly into a madness that gets beyond either shame or self-control. Although both police and magistrates understand the ways of the hair-fetishist, the law does not recognize that he exists. The cutting of hair is merely common assault, and there is no machinery for recognizing and treating the symptoms of a potentially dangerous disease.

There are perverts who find no satisfaction in a girl unless she wears high-heeled shoes or tight corsets. It is only such an alarmingly simple step in the diseased mind of the pervert from the pleasure of a constricted waist to that of a constricted throat. There are men who enjoy dressing up in women's clothes, and who thereby commit an offence against the law. There are also men who enjoy seeing girls dressed in male clothing, and that is in no way an offence against the law as it exists today.

I do not blame a person for having tendencies towards a perversion. But I do blame him for indulging them, and I blame anybody or anything that tends to encourage such indulgence.

The law recognizes that it is an offence to incite a person to perform an illegal act, and I think that all recognizable forms of perversion should be defined in law as illegal acts. The film censors will not permit a man and woman to occupy a bed together unless the man has his feet on the floor. But they will permit scenes of violence that are plainly designed to arouse sadism in the audience. And sadism is the most dangerous of all forms of perversion.

Many of London's worst murders have been the work of sadists. A sadist is a person who derives sexual excitement from cruelty, just as a masochist is a person who is sexually excited by having pain or discomfort inflicted upon him. Far too often the victims of sadists are innocent children—sometimes his own. I would go so far as to assert that I strongly suspect the motives of any man who makes a ritual of chastising his children.

But one cannot avoid a certain amount of sadism in life. It is there in boxing matches, in wrestling shows, in gangster films. The trouble arises when a person—it is usually a man—begins to make a deliberate hobby of thinking about his perversions. Until a few months ago there was a notorious shop-window behind Leicester Square, and another in Shepherd's Market, where, for a shilling per week, one could put a post-

card in a glass frame that was crowded with similar "advertisements." These two particular displays have since been
considerably modified, but there are still dozens of similar—
if smaller—ones around Paddington district, and off the Tottenham Court Road, and in a dozen other parts of London.
This is the sort of advertisement they carry:

(a) "Young man, artistic type, in need of strict dis-
cipline, seeks companion, preferably older, of dominant
personality and habits."

(b) "Female impersonator (amateur) wants instruc-
tion in escapology."

(c) "Bachelor (45) seeks young man, artistic and understanding disposition, to share flat. Nominal rent to right
kind of personality."

These are three actual examples that were taken by Vice
Squad officers from these notice-boards.

It is, as the law stands at present, a waste of time to take
any particular police action about them—except to go around
and administer a little of what in private police slang is known
as "frightening powder" to the proprietor of the show-case in
question. But the fact is that those three advertisements mean:
(a) that a young pervert who finds sexual pleasure in masochism, is blatantly advertising for an elderly sadist to indulge
in mutual perversion: (b) that a man who enjoys dressing up
as a girl wishes somebody to tie him up and indulge in perverted practices; (c) that a homosexual with his own flat
wishes to find a younger homosexual to live with him—rent-free
if, satisfactory.

There are perverts who find pleasure in dressing up themselves and each other in rubber garments, from surgical gloves
to motor-cycling mackintoshes . . . the list is almost bewildering in its assortment. But the fact is that many murders—
particularly child murders—are committed by men who first of
all had a tendency towards sadism, and deliberately provoked

and teased this weakness within themselves, and went out of their way to indulge it—until one day their unhealthy daydreams and erotic thoughts came to the logical, tragical conclusion and they suddenly came back to normal to find themselves kneeling upon the grass, or in the dust of an empty cellar, with a dead child between their hands. I maintain that such a man begins to commit actual murder from the first moment that he begins to indulge his sadistic daydreams, from the instant that he deviates from his normal routine, and begins to buy sadistic novelettes, or to seek out a prostitute or masochistic amateur to share his perverted interests.

Such men are a menace to the safety of our children, and to the moral well-being of London, from the first step they take along the road of perversion. And I believe that anyone who does anything at all towards pandering to such impulses, is equally guilty as an accessory—just as a shopkeeper who sells loaded pistols is guilty of a dangerous offence.

WHATEVER THE PLEASURE-SEEKER IS looking for, London can provide it. The path may stay comparatively level, or it may descend downhill into such pits that even a policeman's hardened stomach may turn a little from what he knows to wait at the end of such a road. . . .

The cinema, for example, is a harmless enough thrill. But what of those lost souls to whom an ordinary film show no longer holds any spark of interest? Vice is like mustard—the more you eat of it, the more you need before you can taste anything at all.

And for such clientele, there are the Secret Cinemas, and the particular, peculiar, plush-seated and dimly lit underworld of such men as Brown Thumb Johnny.

The patrons pay £5. The room is dimly lit. Free drinks tinkle upon a tray. Then the lights go out and a film show begins that would turn the censor purple if he knew.

But he doesn't know. Usually the film is a 16-mm., smuggled in from the Continent, or photographed behind locked doors, to be shown in London's underworld cinemas.

There are at least a dozen such secret studios in London today where films of this type can be seen.

No resplendent doorman stands shouting: "Adults only!" There are never any posters. These places do not advertise. Some taxi-men know where these "blue films" are shown. A few bar-tenders or waiters in certain Soho clubs can tell you. Many of the girls who wait under Piccadilly's street lamps could show you the places where you can, any night, see films with such titles as "Julia Learns the Ropes," "Captive Blonde Girl," "Beauties in Bondage," "Sous La Joupe," "Fifi et Ses Deux Amis."

But mostly the clients come from "Brown Thumb Johnny," London's newest big-money crook. They say he makes at least £6,000 a year. He seldom spends any. He is the new king of the "blue film" racket.

After the police raided the flat of the notorious "Queenie" in Marylebone High Street, and the plain blue vans of New Scotland Yard took away four cabin-trunks filled with quaint costumes and other implements that are the stage props of the "French Circus," together with three haplessly young girls (ages 16-18) who had been among the dazed performers, it was felt at the Yard that we had struck a successful and possibly a death-blow at obscene shows in London.

Clients in all walks of life were discovered upon Queenie's ledgers. Some fled the country. Queenie went to jail.

Then a flat in the West End came under police observation. The Black Maria was wheeled up—and another armload of tainted stage-props was removed to the Police Museum—already well stocked with such bizarre trophies.

When it seemed that the "French Circus" was too risky, the underworld turned to films.

A few months ago two men were sent to prison for six months for "publishing and uttering obscene films," and Detective Sergeant Winston Gardner closed a case that had kept him six months on the trail. Thirty-nine films were destroyed.

Now Brown Thumb Johnny has stepped into the vacancy. He walks with a stained old mackintosh flung across his arm so carelessly that its sleeves usually dangle on the pavement at his heels.

He smokes endlessly. His plump crinkled fingers are caked with nicotine. His fingers are also brown with photographic chemicals. It is from both these that he gets his nickname.

Johnny began as a commercial photographer, attending weddings and twenty-first parties. He had his own darkroom, and made spare-time pin money by developing and printing at cut rates for amateurs.

One such roll of film was of nudes. Johnny developed it. With amazing rapidity the news spread. Soon Johnny found dozens of similar films sent him to be treated.

Commercial firms will never develop a film showing any kind of nude, even if it is supposedly "artistic." They always "regret that the negative was destroyed in the developing process." They would sooner replace your film than get mixed up in it.

Johnny put up his prices. The flow of work surprisingly increased! It was the first inkling to him of the demand for such stuff. He set up his own studio, took photos and advertised them for sale, to "Art Lovers and Students of the Body Beautiful."

Before long he was summoned on charges of sending improper photographs through the post. Police found a file-index of hundreds of names, from all parts of England. Johnny cheerfully paid the maximum fine of £10 on each charge.

He was not abashed by the confiscation of his card-index file. Weeks before he had photographed each card on 8-mm. film, and thus had the whole list of names preserved on a roll of celluloid not much bigger than four pennies placed together.

Clients who read with anxiety of the police raid were soon to receive, with mixed emotions, a letter from Brown Thumb

Johnny, assuring them that the confiscated files did not include *their* name, but that Johnny was troubled whether he should make a clean breast of the whole business. Meanwhile, surely there was a slight matter of £2 outstanding from previous orders?

The money raised made Johnny a rich man. It did not, however, appear to run to a shave, haircut, clean shirt or shoeshine.

Today, friends of his sell sexy French and American magazines. These are nearly all second-hand. Customers who buy such a magazine can sell it back at half-price.

This way Johnny meets potential customers. Scribbled inside many of the second-hand magazines are pencilled messages using a Monomark or similar box-number, and inviting an exchange of letters with the previous reader.

Anybody foolish enough to follow up this "pen-pal" invitation will find himself—or herself—tempted deeper and deeper into obscenities.

Then comes the invitation—to the Blue Show! But not until the victim is utterly committed by his own letters.

These "blue films" are not difficult to get if you know how. They can be purchased openly in Paris and New York. A 16-mm. film of 200 feet, with some such title as "The Blonde Bandit Takes Her Medicine," costs $24 (£8) in New York. Ships' crews bring them over. They are often smuggled in, disguised as unexposed cine-film, and normal duty paid.

Brown Thumb Johnny's clients will pay anything between £3 to £10 each for the hire of such films. Johnny never shows them himself.

He hires the films to little "private groups" that have been organized, via his bookshop, to view them. After being shown to several different groups, the films are sold to some collector.

The French equivalents are slightly more expensive, but usually badly lit.

Clients are soon sated with these suggestive commercially

manufactured films, and begin to demand something stronger. They can have it—at a price!

But these costlier films are not smuggled in. It is easier, and safer, to make them in England. The films are taken under baby floodlights with a 16-mm. cine-camera. Almost any room will do as a studio.

Most of his clients are in Paddington and Chelsea, with a sprinkling of business men who visit London frequently.

For the moment Brown Thumb Johnny is being very clever. He knows the police will catch him with the first mistake he makes. He will be fined and perhaps—it is a big perhaps—be sent to prison for a few months.

Johnny doesn't mind. The worst part of prison, for him, will be the compulsory weekly bath.

And he knows his clients—poor fools—will still be waiting for him when he comes out!

IF SINFUL CINEMAS ARE NOT ENOUGH, there are practitioners of evil who will arrange to raise the Devil himself to be your sulphurous nocturnal playmate!

The practice of Black Magic—of diabolical religious rites in the heart of London—is spreading steadily. There is more active Satan-worship today than ever since the Dark Ages, when witches were publicly burned upon Tower Hill.

When Scotland Yard was asked to help the police of Finland to investigate an outbreak of black magic at Helsingfors, which had resulted in more than forty corpses being stolen from the mortuary and mutilated, the books of black magic found upon the culprits were discovered to have been printed in London. When Aleister Crowley (The Beast 666) died near Brighton, members of black-magic circles of London, Lewes and Shoreham attended his pagan funeral.

When a Sunday in December falls on the 13th day of the

month (as it did in 1953) and is, therefore, the 13th day before Christmas, the moon may shine upon London's rooftops, but, in any case, men and women will congregate at midnight in secret temples of South Kensington, Paddington and—I believe, Bloomsbury, too—to strip off their clothes and worship Satan with ritual and sacrifice that would shame an African savage!

Some firmly believe the world is a battleground between God and Satan, and if they declare themselves with the Devil, he will aid their success in life, and even a certain amount of comfort in Hell, with the chance of being reborn periodically as leaders of earthly wickedness.

Others—probably the majority—attend a Black Mass to see a cheap thrill. They have heard of obscene ceremonies—naked girl "priestesses"—blood sacrifice of cats and goats—lewd flagellations and evil drums.

They do not realize—until it is too late—that in these temples of Satan, brain-stealing herbal incenses and hypnotic devices are mercilessly used—until the man or girl who came just to stare and giggle may find themselves trapped.

On the files of Scotland Yard is one case of a girl, aged twenty-one, who went with her mother to a lecture on Satanism. She was invited to a garden party at the house of a woman calling herself a "High Priestess," who persuaded the girl to sing a "magical invocation," in the process of which the girl was successfully hypnotized.

She did not return home for months. When, with the help of the Yard, her parents finally recovered her, the girl had been hypnotized and exposed to occult obscenities so persistently that she was almost insane. Her own pet dog ran howling in fear from her. It took two years to restore her mind. There was no prosecution, because there was no evidence. The girl had been "willed" to forget how it had happened.

The door to black magic is through the back offices of two or three dusty little London bookshops that specialize in volumes on the occult, diabolism, alchemy. . . . Satan-worshippers also get their new victims among likely-looking students at lectures on spiritualism, necromancy, tribal rites. . . .

There is a house in Lancaster Gate that consists of one-room flatlets. The landlord and his wife occupy the ground floor and basement. Each room has a covered wash-bowl, a rather dispirited bed, a slot-meter gasfire, rickety table and two wooden chairs.

The landlord's wife dabbles in spiritualism, sometimes holds private seances. Her husband is an amateur herbalist. Their flatlets are seldom taken for more than a few days. They are too dingy and untended to be comfortable. Guests come and go.

Among them come and go the Satanists. Down in the cellar is a small doorway—probably, at one time, it was a fireplace. It leads through to the house whose walls adjoin it. The front door of this house faces upon an entirely different street. It is privately owned, and, from its cellar, stairs go to an old-fashioned service lift-shaft, up which a spiral metal staircase ascends and stops at a sliding door, padded with black felt. Beyond this door is a private Temple of Satanism!

Note how subtly the approach has been designed to be eerie and furtive. You go in at one house, down into the cellar, through the narrow hole in the wall, up twisting stairs through almost utter blackness, open a sliding black sound-proof door —and you are suddenly in a large room, sickly with odors from two tall brass braziers. The room is lit dimly by wick lamps, that burn a dark green fat which smells abominable, and seems to have some stupefying power. I think the acrid smell conceals the fact that the "temple" is probably densely sprayed with ether or chloroform.

At one end of the long room is an altar, exactly as in a small church—except that the altar candles are black wax, and the crucifix is head downwards. There are no seats. Around the walls are low divans. Alongside each burns a saucer of dried herbs. Symbols of wizardry are daubed on cloths that

completely cover the walls. Pentagrams and sigils (supposed
to be the magic signs of devils) are on the low ceiling. On the
left of this altar, is a black African idol—the juju, obviously,
of some heathen fertility rite. It is nearly five feet high, squat,
repulsive and obscenely constructed. It is rubbed to a greasy
polish by the ecstatic bare flesh of worshippers.

The horrible cleverness of all this is that—at a cost of probably less than £300—the black magic disciples have set their
stage to capture not merely the adolescent instinct that is in
most of us for "secret societies," but also the adult hunger for
some strong religious impulse, and the immemorial super-
stitious fear of "devils."

The Black Mass—they call it the "Mass of Saint Secaire"—
is a close parody of the Holy Eucharist, with chants and
responses fervently intoned in Latin. It is performed at midnight. The priest is visibly naked beneath his canonical robes.
His clerk is a woman—her dress outwardly an ordinary church
garment, but altered to make it indecent. When the wafers and
the wine (which has been adulterated with "magical drugs"
like vervain) have been consecrated, they are then blas-
phemed and obscenely soiled. The "worshippers" believe these
filthy fragments, concealed in lockets or mixed with wax to
make little images, possess the power to invoke a curse upon
their enemies.

This ceremony of Black Mass is—compared with some—
almost decorous. There is a witchcraft ritual, in which young
girls or susceptible boys are dedicated to Pan, that is indescrib-
able. It is followed by a "fertility ceremony," involving the
African idol.

There is also a "Rite of Abramelin"—supposedly to raise
devils, that requires a naked girl to be bound to the replica of
the church altar.

Chelsea has an "Order of St. Bridget" that meets weekly
for the purpose of mutual flagellation. Initiates are stripped,
their arms tied in a cross behind their backs, and flogged by
"Inquisitors" dressed in monks' cowls, until they "confess."

And there are a growing number of "psychic circles" that begin with harmless spiritualism and gradually seduce the more hysterical and neurotic members towards Satanism.

The difficulty of the police is that, in England, it has never been the duty of the police to suppress religious sects. Nor can they easily get "spies" into the black-magic orgies. For the initiates are cleverly taken, step by step, through various stages of ritual. Only by co-operating whole-heartedly in the early, trivial obscenities, can they win their way into the more vile ceremonies.

Evidence from such witnesses could be made to seem dangerously like that of an "agent provocateur." There is also a very real danger of police witnesses being hypnotized. Not even the London policeman or policewoman can guarantee to be immune, in an atmosphere thick with perfumed ether, throbbing with jungle drums and chants.

Watch the local newspapers. You may see the signs of witchcraft—reports of robberies at churches, where coins in the poorbox are left untouched, but Holy Eucharist wafers and wine, left over from Communion services, are stolen. The more fanatic disciples of Satanism believe that only an apostate priest can consecrate the bread and wine. Unless they can bribe some renegade to perform their travesty of a Mass, they steal the Holy Eucharist to defile in their private ceremonies.

They drive miles out into the country, to make these thefts from lonely little churches. One recently reported was at Yarcombe, Devon, where the horrified vicar found actual remnants of a Black Mass in his church—black candles burned down, the amputated paw of a white kitten on the altar, the prayer-book disfigured, and twelve stone crosses turned upside down.

So, if you have a friend who dabbles in the occult, and who offers, laughingly, to take you to see a ceremony of Black Mass performed—don't go! The laugh may be on you! And it will be a very Satanic chuckle. . . .

THERE IS NOTHING QUITE LIKE THE PUB
in any other part of the world, and no survey of London after
dark would be complete without dealing with this important
side of life in the metropolis. The pub has often been described
as the poor man's club, and at one time this was more or less
true. Today, however, pubs have become social centers for all
classes of society, and some have become as famous as the
coffeehouses of Samuel Johnson's time.

Why do people go to pubs at all? The obvious answer is to
drink, but this is by no means the main reason. If to drink were
the main objective, it is no more expensive, and certainly less
trouble, to drink at home. No, people, or most of them, go to
pubs in search of bustle, gaiety, laughter and a buzz of talk.
Where they find these they are good-humored, tolerant and
well-mannered. Business men meet to discuss their affairs, and
many big deals have been settled in a London pub; the ordi-

nary citizen exchanges his views on any topic of the day, including his views on the government; and sport, especially soccer, is a lively subject for discussion. If a leading politician or football star really wants to know what his fans think about him, then he will find out quickly enough in a London pub.

But a large number of London pubs are more than just meeting-places for individuals. There was a time when a woman in a pub was only there for one purpose, but many of them are now meeting-places for husband and wife, or friends of both sexes. In fact, so important has the pub become as a social center, that in most new housing estates which have been built since the war, a pub has been included in the layout.

To maintain this high standard, there are a large number of "thou-shalt-nots" which face the publican, and here are just a few. He must not:

(*a*) Allow betting in the pub. This is very strictly enforced, and a publican can very soon lose his license if he allows any laxity in this rule.

(*b*) Allow billiards on Sunday. The reason for this is not obvious, as it cannot be more wicked to play the game on Sunday than any other day in the week. It is probably a survival of a strict Sabbatarian approach to the Lord's Day, and, like so many similar rules and regulations, awaits the hand of the reformer.

(*c*) Allow the pub to be used as a brothel. This is a most important rule as there was a time within living memory when certain pubs were used for immoral purposes, and quite unfit places to take one's female relations or friends.

(*d*) Serve liquor to policemen while on duty. Hard luck on a thirsty policeman, maybe, but a very wise precaution.

(*e*) Allow drunkenness, violent, quarrelsome or riotous conduct to take place on his premises. I am not going to pretend that there is no drunkenness in pubs today —there is—but compared with my young days, it is no longer a serious social problem. I well remember the average Saturday night on my beat when the paths were strewn with drunks of both sexes. Fights were a regular feature, and it was quite common to see two women surrounded by a crowd tearing at each other's hair and screaming. Not a pretty sight, I can assure you.

(f) Harbor thieves or reputed thieves, policemen on duty or prostitutes. A pub is a natural meeting-place, and a publican has to be especially careful to ensure that his premises are not used for criminal purposes or soliciting by males or females.

Such are some of the precautions taken to ensure that pubs maintain a high standard of respectability. But, as every policeman knows, there are black spots, and within the Square Mile of Vice, there are places where anything might happen. They are situated off the beaten track, however, and only the too curious, as in the case of some of the night clubs which I have mentioned, are likely to get into any trouble. There are a few pubs, known to the police, which are favored by gangs and other undesirables, and they are best left alone.

I enjoy an evening in a London pub, and like most people, I have my favorites. There is "The Prospect of Whitby" at Wapping Wall, now presided over by that genial host George Broadbent. It is believed that this pub was built in 1543, although the name by which it is known today can only be traced back to 1777. In the upstairs dining room there is a plate on a chair which was occupied by Princess Margaret during a visit. In the same room there is the parrot which "starred" in the film *Treasure Island,* and his specialty today is to screech out, "Pieces of Eight."

"The Mitre," in Ely Place, just off Holborn Circus, was built in 1546 by Bishop William Goodrich for the use of palace

officials. In the parlor is the base of the cherry tree which at
one time marked the boundary between the Bishop's garden
and the part leased to Sir Christopher Hatton, who was appointed Lord Chancellor of England in 1587. The corner
where Dr. Johnson entertained his friends has been preserved,
and round the walls are a number of interesting sketches by
the famous caricaturist, "Spy." A gold-braided porter preserves
traditional dignity and order, and when the gates are closed he
reassures those within with the ancient "Fine night, all's well."

Have you ever visited "Dirty Dick's" in Bishopsgate? This
pub was established in 1745, and was named after Nathaniel
Bentley, who in his time was one of the best-known characters
in the City of London. He became known as "Dirty Dick" on
account of the fund of doubtful stories which he always had at
his command. In the corner of the basement bar there is a
lucky cat—a real dried-up cat. After putting a coin or two in
the charity box you are expected to touch the cat for luck.
Hanging all around are relics of bygone days: more dried cats,
old umbrellas, hats, lamps, drinking vessels, and so on, all
thick with the dirt and dust of ages. This pub is certainly
worth a visit.

A pub of quite a different type is "The Fitzroy Tavern," in
Charlotte Street, just off Tottenham Court Road. It is truly an
amazing place, and often is so crowded that the uniformed
man on the door has to announce, "Sorry, house full." I am
assured that there is every naval cap tally of the British Royal
Navy displayed on the walls, and also scores of other tallys
from foreign ships. Other parts are adorned by an almost
complete set of Army identification badges, many dating back
to the First World War. Thirty years ago a "Pennies from
Heaven Party" for children was started, and during every
evening ever since a box is passed round and the customers
drop a coin or two in. This is totaled up on the bar counter,
and the proprietor usually makes the amount up to a level
note. The sum is then wrapped in colored paper in which a
piece of cork is placed to which a large tack is fixed. Then,

anyone who cares will throw the package up to the ceiling where it remains till December, when some well-known actor or actress will preside over the ceremony of getting all the packets down. The average amount collected is in the region of £600, and with this a party is held for 500 poor children.

Lastly, among my many favorites, is the "George Inn," just off Borough High Street, near London Bridge. It was rebuilt in 1676 after being destroyed by the Great Fire of London, and is one of the few remaining specimens of an old-time inn, with galleries round its inner court. Every year the birthday of Shakespeare is made an occasion for a special production by one of the many amateur societies in London.

London's pubs are, indeed, a rich store of history and centers of healthy conviviality. I have only mentioned a few, but I hope I have said enough to persuade you to make your own tours of discovery.

Part Two

THE STOP-AT-NOTHING CROOKS

The Master Minds of Crime

WHEN GREY TOBY CAME OUT OF
Dartmoor he was ambitious to return to the smash-and-grab
game. I had been in charge of the Flying Squad when, after a
smash-and-grab job, we put Grey Toby into Dartmoor for
seven years. He had not been with the team who actually did
the raid, but he planned it. In his house at Islington (apart
from proceeds of another burglary) we found crucibles glow-
ing hot ready to melt down the stuff; a handful of platinum
ring-shanks was waiting there to receive, re-set and disguise
the stolen stones when his boys fetched the loot in.

The boys did not bring it in. They finished up with their
big Bentley against the railings beyond Knightsbridge, and a
Squad car bumper-bar nuzzling their front fender. Their
driver, a bright-eyed consumptive Scots boy named "Grudie,"
had tuned the Bentley until he could change down into third
gear at seventy for extra acceleration. He imagined himself to
be the best driver in London.

But there were thirty Flying Squad drivers, at least, who

could give him points. It was one of these who out-drove, out-maneuvered and out-nerved Grudie, with no more than a flying V-8 to compare with the thieves' £4,000 Bentley. That was the end of Grey Toby's smash-and-grab team.

Grey Toby had always worked everything out, careful as a scientist. He personally chose the jeweler's to be "done." He plotted the "escape map," timed the traffic lights with a stop-watch, made Grudie memorize the sharp right-hand turns, being easier at high speeds than left-hand turns.

He knew which days the big delivery trucks would be coming to block up the narrow streets. He had special tires to grip the road on wet days.

He produced the scheme of using two identical, big, open tourers. One was registered in his name and he used it bla-tantly. The other was provincially registered, and hidden. This was the "hotted-up" job.

Four or five days before the smash-and-grab was to be done, the provincial "stooge," who had the second car regis-tered in his name out in the country, would report it "stolen." The local police never stood a chance of finding it because it was already hidden in London's West End, waiting for the big day.

Then, out it would come, with number plate artistically and indecipherably mud-splashed. The smash-and-grab would be done, the car would scream recklessly away and, in a matter of minutes, be abandoned, while the "innocent" twin laid a false trail across London.

When the Squad cars caught up with the second car, its driver was always righteously indignant and had a perfect alibi. At the exact time of the robbery, he had usually been having his tanks filled up at a respectable garage!

That was the *modus operandi* and it worked two or three times—until the inevitable day when it didn't!

Grey Toby did every day of his seven years. He came out, not owing society a minute of good conduct remission, and unrepentedly ready to start where he left off.

But in London, now, the golden days of smash-and-grab

teams have departed. "We're leaving it alone these days, Toby," he was told curtly, when he tried to get a team together.

Grey Toby had to find new recruits among the "tearaways," the boastful young spivs who will do anything rather than admit to being "milky." He decided that when the time came to smash the jeweler's window, he would do it himself. He picked a quick youngster for the job of tying up the shop door, so that the jeweler and his staff could not rush out.

He could not do his elaborate car-swapping job this time, so he did the next best thing. He made his young driver practice on a fast, American-type car and, on the day planned for the theft, he had another young spiv steal a similar car from Grosvenor Square for the job.

He took another member of the milk-bar gang in the car with him—a husky lad of twenty-two—to stand by, keep the car doors open and be ready to cosh any passer-by who tried to interfere with the escape.

At the appointed day and time the young gangster responsible for tying the door did his bit. The husky hooligan with the cosh stood ready. The car driver had his engine revving beautifully in low gear and, by adroit clutch-work, was just sidling along the curb edge, ready for a jump getaway.

Like the cool professional he was, Grey Toby swung his iron bar just right. The big window took the blow and was immediately covered with a glittering spiderweb of splinters. Toby swung again—more of a tap than a heavy blow—and the plate-glass window fell with a boom.

There was no protective grille. Grey Toby dropped the iron bar and started to plunge his hands into the contents of the window—then he realized there was a second plate-glass window that had been invisible. With a curse he stooped, retrieved the bar, struck again—and the big, protecting glass simply swung with the blow like a brass gong. It was hinged at the top. He hit it again and again, broke a piece off and managed to grab a handful of stuff.

Grey Toby and his hulking bodyguard scrambled frantically through the crowd and into the car. The youth who had tied the jeweler's door had to be abandoned, gibbering with fear.

The kid at the wheel drove like a lunatic. He was scared. Keeping cool is easy to dream about, but things had begun to go wrong, and that's what scares them. The big, muscular chap lost his nerve completely. It is nearly always the bully type that does.

"This way," he screamed, "turn this way," as the car whirled and dodged. Finally he grabbed the driver's hair in his panic, and the car ran on to the pavement. Despite all this, Grey Toby got away.

When the police called at his lodgings that night he was indignant. "Who, me?" he said. "Just because I've come out of stir, you think . . ."

They broke the news to him gently. There was an electric "eye" in the jeweler's window. When he broke the glass and put his hand through, the machine took his photograph. "Quite a good one, too, Toby," said the C.I.D. sergeant placidly, "but not as good as your photo in the Criminal Record Office."

When charged, Grey Toby is on record as having said sadly: "Blimey, you can't keep up with things, these days— I mean, a thief hardly stands a sporting chance."

Wrong in so many things, Grey Toby was dead right there.

There is another "Master-Mind" of London's active underworld who is also due for a disappointment shortly, as was Grey Toby—and the Gelignite Gang who had a dazzling run of success before being picked up in London recently. We will call him the "Dormouse," which is near enough to his actual underworld nickname to be recognizable in certain parts of Soho.

He is a gray-haired, middle-aged little man. He sits with shoulders hunched, and blinks quickly behind gold-rimmed, old-fashioned spectacles. His small, soft hands are pressed together beneath his chin as he thinks. He thinks to some purpose. He has been the master-planner behind several big thefts in the past ten years, but has never yet been convicted.

A few years before the war, the Dormouse was a respected cashier with a London firm. Some cash was missed. They couldn't prove the Dormouse took it. But they gave him a chance to resign—and he did, without a murmur.

He found a job as cashier in a Soho night club, not far from Leicester Square. He used to sit there, blinking and harmless-looking, like a tiny gray squirrel in its cage, handling the bills, giving change to waiters. Whenever he got a chance, his bright little eyes used to dart to and fro, watching the customers at the tables. . . .

After a few months, we began to get a lot of successful robberies on West End flats, houses, hotel suites. Always jewels and furs were stolen. Every time Flying Squad men went to talk to the victims, the same story kept reappearing: "No, we were out at the time of the robbery . . . we'd gone to the XX Club. . . ."

I went to have a talk with my friend who runs the XX Club, which the *élite* of society patronized for champagne suppers. I went through his staff with a magnifying glass. They all seemed honest, as far as one could tell.

"And who's that little bloke in the corner?" I asked.

"He's my new cashier—harmless little chap—an absolute treasure!" That was my first meeting with the Dormouse.

I had him checked, as routine. No criminal record. Nothing but that one whisper of suspicion against him in the past. It seemed hardly fair to mention it. But when I did mention it, and the Dormouse was moved on from the XX Club, the robberies stopped.

It was clear what had happened. The Dormouse had kept his eyes open. When Lady Glitter came to the XX Club wearing a small fortune in diamonds, the Dormouse took careful note. During the afternoons, before work, he checked up on Lady Glitter.

Next time Lady Glitter swept into the XX Club, the mild

eyes of the Dormouse dwelt upon her throat. Emeralds to-night! Where, then, were the diamonds? The answer was obvious—they were at home, and Lady Glitter, equally obviously, was not.

The Dormouse's tiny, furtive paw reached out for the telephone. "Hello, Tommy—I say, be a pal and see if I left the gas-fire on in my room, will you?" A brief laugh. "Yes, I know that's about the seventeenth time this month. . . . Thanks, Tommy . . . 'bye." And the Dormouse rang off.

The message would be whisked off like lightning to the little team of expert burglars who were impatiently awaiting it. "The Dormouse says Number 17." And when Lady Glitter arrived back at her tasteful little Mayfair town-flat, she would find it skilfully burgled—and usually—the diamonds gone!

So we knew how the Dormouse had worked his jobs. But it was difficult to prove. Even when the thieves were, from time to time, arrested, they wouldn't squeal. Another team of burglars was only too anxious to make use of the Dormouse's red-hot, reliable tips. The underworld would have cheerfully massacred the squealer who spoiled that little game.

So the Dormouse became unemployed. We watched him like hawks. He didn't spend too much money, never got drunk, never boasted to girls how clever he was. He got another quiet little job as a clerk in a bookmaker's office, and did a bit of betting, which at once made it extremely difficult to keep accurate check on his financial state.

Then the Dormouse started to take a keen interest in literature. The girl on the railway station bookstall began to say, "Good morning, sir," very respectfully to the Dormouse. All the glossy, expensive magazines that were devoted to photographs and gossipy paragraphs about what the rich are doing, and snapshots of Lord This and The Hon. Daphne That, perched grinning on shooting-sticks . . . all such magazines, the Dormouse purchased and studied devoutly.

Sometimes, with a fat little gold pencil, he would mark a paragraph.

It was shortly after the Dormouse had become such an ardent reader of: *Tatler, Hare & Hounds, The Sketch & Sphere, The Bystander, Country Life,* and *Illustrated London News,* etc., that the big outcrop of successful country house robberies began, around London. . . . Many of these were in provincial police districts, and were not always Scotland Yard's concern. Sometimes the thieves were arrested. But they never grassed on the Dormouse. A prison sentence does not last forever, and when a burglar emerges, he wishes to be sure of still receiving good tips of where the best stuff is to be found, and when. So, for the time being, the Dormouse has enjoyed a good run.

But he has made two mistakes. The first was after a particularly daring and successful robbery of a valuable load of silver ingots from a London district airport, the Dormouse exhibited his first quirk of humor, and—indeed—of humanity at all.

He and his bookmaker boss (though who today employs whom is not entirely clear) set up their joint, at the next race meeting, under the banner: "NICK SILVER—Safe as Bullion!"

This caused a deal of amusement in the underworld. But to me it looked like the beginning of the end for the Dormouse. He had made his first mistake—he had boasted! Recently I hear he boasted again. Funny how these smart boys can never resist it. The other mistakes will soon follow, for they invariably do.

That's the trouble with Master Minds. Even the Electronic Brain Machine at Manchester University, which is the biggest and most miraculous calculating machine in the world, can have its breakdowns, and therefore make mistakes. But you can't take a screwdriver to a Master Mind of Crime. Let him make just one mistake—and he's finished.

It was that way with "Sneery Harry," who was for a long time the master-planner behind blackmail in London. Harry had nothing in common with the Dormouse, except perhaps a cool and ruthless brain. He was a big man, with curly brown hair, and a wide, cruel mouth like a film gangster. He played the dirty blackmail game with skill but no mercy.

It was Harry who invented the trick of keeping watch upon certain houses of sin and following the prosperous-looking clients home, or tracing their car license-plates. He also had pale, lisping young men planted in West End turkish baths. Sneery Harry was undoubtedly a devil.

Then he made a mistake, when—like all "master minds"— he had begun to think he couldn't. He got ten years. He came out and tried to begin again. But in crime you can't begin again. And Sneery Harry is inside the tall walls again as I write. He got another ten years. When he finally comes out, he will be old, white-haired and washed up. Just like the Dormouse will be, quite soon.

THERE ARE ALL SORTS OF VIOLENCE IN London's night streets—some is drunken, some vicious and some is done in despair. But the Hymie Brothers make violence their business, and with them it has become very Big Business indeed! If Al Capone had known the Hymie Brothers, he would have made them rich men. Or corpses.

You probably never heard of Big Hymie and Little Hymie. But all the underworld of London knows them. So does Scotland Yard.

They live among the narrow streets and shadowy pavements around Aldgate Pump. Little Hymie keeps a sort of club, not far away. It used to have a respectable club license, but the police took this away in 1948. Since then, it has been just a couple of fairly large rooms, up some stairs next to a tailorshop, down a little cul-de-sac. In these rooms, some of the worst thugs in London sit every night around a blazing fire, swap cigarettes and boasts, and show each other the absurd little conjuring tricks that are the current craze among the city's lay-abouts.

Some of them are broken-nosed and razor-slashed. All have police records. But they fall into respectful silence whenever Big Hymie or Little Hymie begins to speak.

If you are a big London bookmaker, a gambler or black-market operator, you will need to know the Hymie Brothers. If somebody owes you money on a gamble, or a shady deal, and you cannot persuade him to pay, it is no use writing to your solicitor. The gambler would plead the Gaming Act. The black-market shark would laugh in your face. You take your problem to the Hymie Brothers, who are London's most blood-curdling debt-collectors. They trade in terror!

Big Hymie is just over six-feet tall. He has huge, oxen shoulders, and, with his overcoat on, has to walk through the door one shoulder at a time. He has curly, auburn hair, and a thin red razor stripe across his cheek, as if somebody had been scribbling upon his skin with a child's pink crayon. He wears number eleven shoes, and his folded fist is the size of a turnip. Amputated at the wrist and thrown on to butcher's scales, the fist of Big Hymie would probably weigh well over half a stone!

His brother, Little Hymie, is only just under average height, but he seems a dwarf alongside Big Hymie. He wears rimless spectacles, sumptuously tailored dark worsted suits, and polished shoes upon which he minces like a dancer. His hair is sleek with oil, but going slightly grey. Big Hymie's hair always looks, by contrast, like a red-brown chrysanthemum.

You might live your entire life in London—even in Aldgate —and never know the Hymie Brothers. If you jostled them in the street, they would step back, feel instinctively to see their money was all right, and pass on. If you wanted to argue in a pub with Big Hymie, he would shake his head with a sad little, cold smile and say: "I've nothin' to say to you, chum!" Big Hymie will seldom make a threatening gesture unless somebody first puts £50 in his pocket.

But there is one certain way to meet the Hymie Brothers professionally. Supposing you open a credit account with—say—Mr. Harry Auchbauch, the well-known West End bookmaker. By the end of a few weeks you have lost, perhaps, £2,000. Mr. Auchbauch threatens to sue. You smile blandly and say: "I shall plead the Gaming Act." Mr. Auchbauch knows that, under this Act, the law refuses to enforce any debt that arises from gambling.

So, there it is. The courts will not help Mr. Auchbauch to get his £2,000. But the Hymie Brothers will . . . for twenty-five per cent.

For two or three days they do not approach you. They are making inquiries—"finding the strength of you"—as they would put it. They want to know if you have the money, if your wife has a fur coat, a diamond ring, if you own the presentable car that you drive, the house you live in. Little Hymie arranges this. A few discreet inquiries are made in your district. Any debt-collecting agency knows this part of the routine.

Along the dark little cul-de-sac and up the bleak wooden stairs to the place that was once Little Hymie's club, come the reports. . . . "His wife's got a nice two-carat groin [diamond ring], and he flashes a heavy gold fag-case. They seem to be spending plenty!" That does it. Big Hymie and Little Hymie are about to pay you a call!

You are having dinner at an expensive restaurant. Two men walk in. One of them dances along on little polished feet, his rimless spectacles twinkling purposefully. The other walks stolidly, wrists loosely at his sides.

They walk straight to your table, and greet you amiably. "Why, hello, there!" says Big Hymie, huskily. He yanks you playfully from your chair. He has you by the tie, and you cannot breathe. There is a silvery flash, under your popping eyes, and you fall back into your chair with a thud.

Big Hymie has slashed off your tie, just short of the Adam's apple. He chuckles. The waiters and other diners watch and wonder. They can't decide yet if it is a clumsy joke or not. "Next time," says Big Hymie conversationally, "it could be an inch higher, couldn't it?"

Little Hymie has meanwhile thoughtfully picked your wine-bottle from its silver ice-bin. Just as thoughtfully, he puts it back, upside down. "Bad habit to get into, chum," he says loudly. "Can't afford to drink stuff like that, when you owe so much money! Bookie's account, isn't it?" He shakes his sleek little head reproachfully. "Bad, that, chum. Not sporting. Get it paid, I'd advise. After all, you can't take it with you if you die, can you?"

Big Hymie thrusts his enormous, red and purple fist under your nose. "Look where I bruised myself," he says. "Must have hit something." He treads on your toe with a shoe like a week-end suitcase. Little Hymie lays a hand on his big arm, and there is a sparkle of diamonds from the rings on his plump little fingers. "We'll see our chum when he's finished his dinner, brother," he says. "Mustn't interfere with his appetite."

Then, in a silence that has fallen upon the restaurant like a snowstorm, Big Hymie and Little Hymie leisurely walk out. And upon the faces of each brother lurks a little, tight smile. They might well smile. The incident has probably earned them £500. Could Danny Kaye earn more?

Of course, if you are stubborn, then all London becomes like a haunted room. In the silent night street, you go to your car. Its tires are slashed. And suddenly, every tall shadow seems to be Big Hymie. You dare not go to the race tracks, to the greyhounds, to wrestling matches, or take a walk alone. It is a battle between you and terror.

There was a tailor near the Charing Cross Road who got involved in a deal for black-market cloth and didn't pay. One Sunday night, when his shop was shut, Big Hymie took a jerrican of acid, and Little Hymie carried a thin-shanked stirrup-pump.

They squirted his entire stock with acid, through the letter-box. When the victim came to his shop on Monday morning, he found a strong smell of fumes and a few tatters of sizzling thread. That was all he had left.

A car-dealer on Warren Street had four brand-new Austin limousine cars that he bought instead of paying a certain debt. Somebody poured a two-lb. packet of granulated sugar into the petrol tank of each car. The resultant mess, after the engines had run for a few minutes, would have made Lord Nuffield weep.

Why do the victims not go to the police and demand protection? The amazing thing is that they usually do not. Even if they did, there are crazy young hoodlums of the underworld, hungry to make a reputation for being tough, who will slash your face for £25, though they know that they will be arrested within a very short time of doing it!

These types of lads are the ones who are flattered to sit in Little Hymie's club, sip tea and accept a cigarette, listen awed to tales of villainy, gape at the fat white bankrolls that the Hymie Brothers stuff nonchalantly into their trouser fob-pockets, and risk two years imprisonment for a handful of £1 notes and a word of praise from those two subtle arch-villains and psychologists in terror, the Hymie Brothers!

I know the Hymie Brothers well. I arrested Big Hymie once, on a charge of inflicting grievous bodily harm. He had broken both a man's arms with an iron bar.

But there is one good thing I can, from my own experience, say of Big Hymie and Little Hymie—they have never yet stepped outside the underworld in their activities. If you have been sloshed by Big Hymie, or threatened blandly by Little Hymie, the chances are that you—in your own small way—are as big a villain as themselves! For they only work where the law will not go.

IN ONE TWELVE MONTHS SCOTLAND YARD confiscated 2,400 fire arms, including 1,613 pistols and revolvers and 96,700 live bullets and small bombs. There are enough lawless guns in London's underworld today to start a revolution.

But there are few gunmen. Only nineteen armed robberies among London's crowded streets and suburbs in 1952. New York exceeds this every day.

Why? I know dozens of crooks in London who carry guns. But they will never be real killers. I have tackled many gunmen in my service with the Yard. And I think most experienced policemen will agree that the true gunman falls into as recognizable a pattern as a tiger with its stripes.

He is under thirty. His eyes are gray. Unless he is insane, the brown-eyed criminal does not carry a gun with intent to use it. He may think he does. But the show-down proves him wrong. The man who shoots to kill has gray eyes. I have never known a fat gunman, nor an athletic one. Nor one who was popular with his underworld friends.

The true gunman is always slender, with agitated appearance, like a man who has been kept waiting. He is solitary. Also, he loves his gun. He cleans it frequently. When I arrested the gunman who did London's first daylight armed robbery of a jeweler's in Oxford Street he was busy loading his gun in his bedroom. He had polished every cartridge until it glittered. If he hadn't been so particular his gun might have been loaded when we burst in.

There was a killer who tried to shoot me in a taxi ride. When I got him to the station we found oil smears on his handkerchief. He had been cleaning his gun a few minutes before he was arrested.

Both these men had gray eyes.

And when the notorious Jenkins gang stole the guns that led them to the gallows, they stole enough cleaning stuff, oil, brushes and flannel, to supply a platoon of soldiers. Jenkins, the de Antiquis killer, had gray eyes.

You can easily buy a gun in London's underworld; £5 will buy you a big revolver, £10 will get a slender automatic pistol to fit the pocket. They are war souvenirs, or smuggled in from France, Belgium, Eire.

And with a gun, the crook—you might think—has a bigger advantage in London than any other capital city of the world. The police are unarmed. London goes about its daily affairs without guns. Less than ten citizens in every million are permitted to carry pistols in the streets.

The average cashier, who collects his big payroll from the banks on Thursdays or Fridays, may be permitted to carry a gun. But it is nearly always an ungainly, short-muzzled gun, with fluff in the chambers and grease in the barrel. Nobody bothers to clean it.

Seven cashiers out of ten could not hit a doorway at ten paces. But still the gunman hesitates. And I think I can tell you why.

It is because every man in the underworld of London knows that if he pulls his gun on a policeman, he must shoot to kill. There is no alternative. Every police officer who meets a criminal with a gun, will go in bare-handed and try to take it from him. Sometimes the policeman succeeds. Sometimes he dies. But there is never a time when he does not try.

I had to do it three times, in my twenty-eight years. Some policemen do it more often. Others, mercifully, never at all. But wherever they walk their beats, day or night, they wait ready to do this dangerous job.

And the criminals know that in London—and in all England —a loaded revolver is less use than a water-pistol in evading arrest. We have never once failed to arrest a crook who has shot a policeman. We just don't go to bed until he is in the cells, with his boots off, and his gun in the C.I.D. room.

I have seen dozens of guns taken recently from criminals— mostly youths. Home-made guns and war souvenirs. I have seen automatic pistols with photos of bathing beauties on the handles. I have seen revolvers fixed with flashlights for shooting policemen in the dark. But they are seldom used. Nor will they be. The gunman in London doesn't stand a chance. There are 16,000 men in the Metropolitan Police. He cannot shoot them all.

But if you should happen to meet a thief with a gun, here are some rules:

Never try to rush him. The more nervous and young he looks, the more likely he is to shoot you.

The smartest thing to do is give him what he wants—but make sure you get a good, clear description of him. Be certain you can pick him out again.

If you *must* be a hero at all costs, then these are the professional ways to tackle a gunman.

If he is at close range. See if the hammer of the gun is cocked. If it is, the man is really dangerous. If not, you can grab the chamber (the part that holds the bullets and turns at each shot). While you do this, he cannot shoot. Never try this with an automatic pistol.

If he is the length of a room away. Throw things. Anything will do—books, cushions, the clock, coins from your pocket.

It is much harder than people think, to shoot accurately with a revolver. You stand a chance, if you advance behind a barrage of missiles, which can be surprisingly disconcerting to a gunman.

But remember, it's only a chance. And for the average citizen, the best advice is: Get a description, and leave the rest to the police. If you can describe him, you will be certain to meet him again. But next time the gun will not be pointing at you. It will lie on the barrister's table, and the gunman will be in the dock.

"**P**ITY YOU WASN'T HERE LAST NIGHT, Mr. Fabian," said the barman. "You never seen such a mess as those villains made of that girl!"

"What villains?" I said. We were in a bar behind Deman Street.

"King's Cross boys, I believe they were, Mr. Fabian." The barman mopped up some spilt beer with his bar-cloth and dabbled it thoughtfully on my sleeve. "She was at that table just behind you, when these three villains come in.

"They take no notice of her—never a glance at this girl, though she's gone as white as my apron when they come in. The boss of 'em orders a bottle of brandy and three pints of beer.

"These villains drink their beer. Then this boss chap pours the whole bottle of brandy into his empty tankard.

"He goes across to this girl. 'Have a drink, Rabbit,' he says, and tips it all over her. Face, hair, clothes—the lot!"

The barman blinked at me. "Ever get neat brandy in your eyes, Mr. Fabian? Well, she starts to scream, claws at her eyeballs. He just grins. He takes out his cigarette-lighter and calmly sets her off like a Christmas pudding!

" 'You can tell the bogeys about that, too!' he says. Then the three of them walk out."

"She was a nark, was she?"

"Must've been, Mr. Fabian. But I mean—blimey—that's a diabolical thing to do—even to a nark!"

"It's not exactly original," I said. "Fat Bobby who ran the Taxi Pirates, did the same thing to a nark a few years back—only he used petrol."

"Blimey," said the barman, "nobody loves a nark, eh?"

He was right. In the underworld of London, the nark is seldom the cringing coward he is usually pictured as being. The nark needs to be very brave indeed.

At Scotland Yard is an official fund which is replenished every year, called "The Information Fund." It exists to reward and encourage narks. A nark—or "grass," as they are also called—can earn £25 or more by telling of a smash-and-grab plot, or the hiding-place of a badly wanted man. A small job may pay only a few shillings. But a big robbery can be worth hundreds of pounds to the nark, from insurance rewards, which the police collect for him. The nark gets ten per cent of the insured value, which is often more than the stuff is worth to the thief.

So, as he moves through the jungle of London's underworld, an alert detective can often pick up a furtive whisper: "Psst! You'll find that stolen stuff under the flagstones in Brixton Nellie's wash-house!" It is the voice of the Nark.

"Acting on information received," says the detective in the witness-box, "I went to Brixton Nellie's, and told her I had reason to believe. . . ."

The nark's name is never divulged, by the police. Having bestowed his Judas kiss he gets his money, signs for it over a twopenny stamp at police headquarters, in the presence of a senior police officer who had nothing to do with the case.

Often I've picked up a half-fainting man or woman in Soho and rushed them to hospital in the Hurry-Up Wagon—as the underworld calls the police van that waits in Piccadilly—with razor-slash from cheekbone to mouth-corner.

This is the "mark of the nark." The aim is to end the cut at the edge of the mouth, so the lips become a continuation of the gash. This seldom heals straight, but leaves a twisted, permanent disfigurement. The men who live on immoral earnings of women, make a specialty of this "punishment."

Despite this horrible possibility, many an ordinary thief will turn informer against a ponce, and decline any reward. In the same way, sex-offenders against children can hope for no shelter from the underworld. Even a "ponce" will shop them.

Once, a man who had four convictions for inflicting grievous bodily harm, told me: "Fair's fair, Guv'nor, and I don't mind a bit of straight villainy, as you know, but that geezer they call Benny the Wire 'as started creeping around Aldgate, pretendin' he's a welfare bloke, and stealing purses from families that don't have more'n a few bob, Guv! That lark ain't on, is it?"

I have also, at the other extreme, had information given to me deliberately to lure the Flying Squad to Tottenham, and thus leave the way clear for a robbery attempt in Forest Hill.

Today, in London, there are half a dozen big-time narks who spy on the underworld for their own profit. They even employ underling narks. Mostly, they specialize in betraying thefts of valuables. They will not move until the insurance company has published its reward in the newspapers. I caught the Mayfair Boys, with £16,000-worth of stolen jewelry, from what a nark told me.

Some thieves will turn nark because they feel they have been cheated of their fair share from a robery. I know one nark who runs terrible risks, just for the thrill of feeling he has power to send men to prison!

Women make good narks. They have less sense of loyalty than men.

There is a woman in Shepherd's Bush who keeps a lodging-

house. It is always full of thieves. She is a big, motherly
woman, with hair dyed pillar-box red and a voice like a fog-
horn. She uses scent that smells like the disinfectant in a
swimming-bath. For hours after she visits a police station you
can detect it, and while she's there her voice makes the walls
quiver. We used to have a saying: "Call yourself a detective?
You couldn't even tell if Kiphouse Florrie was in the room!"

Florrie is a pitiless nark. Some of the men in her lodging-
house are her lovers. When she gets tired of them, Florrie
will "shop" them mercilessly. There is always a lot of talk
about "getting Florrie done," but it has never actually happened.

One of the best narks in London was called Hoppy. He sold
newspapers near Piccadilly. Hoppy knew everything. He was
a one-man C.I.D.

But the meanest nark I ever met was a fellow called "Holey
Nose." He had nostrils you could have hidden half a dozen
walnuts in. He was a curbside seller of worthless, catchpenny
articles, known in thieves' slang as "flash." His father had been
an honest Armenian, but Holey Nose spoke broadest Cockney
down both barrels.

He came into the C.I.D. room where I was a very new,
eager young probationary detective. "I want to see the Head
Lad," he said. The "Head Lad" is the divisional detective
inspector.

"What for?"

He eyed me learily. "Like to do y'self a bit o' good, matie?
I got the straight info on a screwing job. Might be worth a nice
bit, eh?"

"What sort of robbery?" I said.

He winked. "Smashin' load o' tom, matie! Worth fifty ton,
if a nicker!"

"Sit down," I said, "and have a cigarette!" Information
about the theft of jewelry worth £5,000, was certainly interesting.

Holey Nose looked with disdain at the Woodbine, but lit

it. "First thing yer do, matie," he said patronizingly, "is lumber this geezer. . . ." He told me the name and description of the man I was to arrest, and the "lushes," or public houses, where I was most likely to find him.

"Had it orf proper, he has," he said, and told the address of the flat in Chesterfield Street, Mayfair, where the robbery had happened. I knew of it. The loss had been reported only three hours before. It wasn't in the newspapers yet. "He'll 'ave the gear on hisself, like as not," said Holey Nose, authoritatively.

I made the arrest, brought the surprised thief to the police station, searched him and found some stolen jewelry in his pocket. It was a ring worth £300. He would not tell me where the rest was.

"Leave it to me, matie," said Holey Nose. "You fix his bail, see! Then let me talk to this geezer in his cell, before you bail him. Pal o' mine, he is. I'll tell him I've sprung 'is bail and persuade 'im to show me where the rest of that stolen gear is!"

Holey Nose was a householder. We let him stand bail, and permitted him to see the thief in the cell. When the two men were alone, Holey Nose took £5 from the man he had betrayed, on the promise that for this sum, Detective Fabian had consented to be bribed to arrange bail! The £5, of course, went into Holey Nose's pocket, and was never seen again.

As soon as he got the man outside, Holey Nose, good as his word, persuaded the man to tell him where the rest of the stolen jewelry was hidden.

"Leave it to me," he told his victim, "I'll flog it for you, an' you can give me a few quid for my trouble!" He added: "Forget your bail—here's a ticket for Dublin. You skip the country, matie!"

Then he phoned me. "That geezer's goin' to hop his bail, matie," he said. "If you pinch him now, you'll find he's got a ticket for Dublin!"

We arrested the man again, at the airport, after he failed

to appear in court next day. He did have a ticket to Dublin.
He got three years. Holey Nose got £25 from the Information
Fund, for which he duly signed. Then he went to live with the
wife of the man he had betrayed!

We left them to their horrid joys for a few weeks. Then I
arrested Mr. Holey Nose with some of the stolen jewelry on
him, about which he had "forgotten" to tell us.

He got two years for receiving. And when he held out his
chipped cocoa mug in his cell-door, for the Good Conduct man
who was dishing out helpings, he came face to face with the
man he had betrayed. The burglar quietly took Holey Nose's
sharp-edged cocoa mug, and thrust the jagged tin into Holey
Nose's face, with a twist of the wrist not unlike a housewife
cutting biscuit-shapes out of flattened dough.

He lost all his good conduct marks, but considered it
worth that. For what were a few good conduct marks, compared with what Holey Nose suffered? His cheek looked like
the Severn Tunnel.

Yes, it's a dangerous game, being a nark!

I HAD JUST WALKED INTO SAVILE ROW
Police Station when the duty inspector said: "Look what we've
got here, Bob." Two young boys were stood by his desk,
blinking defiantly in the harsh light of the charge office, and
a struggling girl was being taken upstairs by a smart young
policewoman. It was Saturday night, and, as London's West
End traffic whirled outside, I looked at the two lads. They
were about fifteen years old, and each wore the outfit of the
London spiv—drape jacket, vivid shoes with soles as thick as
match-boxes, trousers hitched high to display red-and-yellow
socks, and bright bow ties. Here, in this costume, are all the
ingredients of exhibitionism—peacocks strutting to attract
attention.

On the charge-room sergeant's desk were piled the contents
of their pockets: cigarette cases, lighters, money, handkerchiefs—and a spiked knuckle-duster. There was also a strange

pocket-knife. It looked foreign, and had a metal button set in one side. I pressed the little button and out flicked a wicked, four-inch dagger-blade that shone in the light.

"What are they in for?" I asked.

He shrugged. "Oh, the usual. They hang around a late-night milk-bar and wait until they see a drunk. Then the girl plays her part by pestering him. Then these two bright beauties jump him with knives and coshes on the pretence that he's insulted their girl friend."

"And rob him, and run off," I nodded. "We used to get a bit of these around the Elephant, but one doesn't expect children to be doing it somehow."

"Don't call these horrors children, Bob," said the inspector. "These are a couple of the Eagle Gang, and that little trollop upstairs is one of their 'molls.'" He went on, "We've had her in twice before—twice and she isn't sixteen yet."

We were interrupted by one of the constables who was searching the boys. "Take off your jackets," he ordered, and as they obeyed sullenly they displayed aluminum shields from wrist to elbow under their shirts.

"Look at that," said the inspector, "they think they're really tough when they've got their armor on. When they've grown up a bit they may discover, as some of their older brothers have, that those gadgets may stop knives, razors and bike-chains, but a tap with a constable's baton will still give 'em a fine enough headache."

The two young gangsters glowered.

"Did you see this, sir?" said the sergeant. He held up a heavy finger-ring embossed with a sharpened hook. "They've got all the gear, haven't they?"

The constable who was examining the jackets suddenly swore softly and sucked at his finger. He had ripped it on a fish-hook sewn with half a dozen others on the right jacket-sleeve near the cuff buttons. The boy who owned the jacket grinned savagely.

"They use 'em, too, Bob," said the inspector. "There was a

girl taken into hospital in Hoxton not long ago. Only about fourteen—she lost half her cheek—raw to the bone, shredded away on sleeve-hooks. Some young villain had leant against her in a milk-bar gang fight and stroked her face away!"

I went upstairs to the women's charge-room, where the girl —Deborah—was lolling insolently in a chair, her nylon legs crossed. The policewoman was sorting through the girl's handbag. I took another look at Deborah. Her pancake make-up tide-marked abruptly at her chin. Her shoes were ankle-strap, and her nail-ends black under red varnish. In the revealing light of the police station she looked unwholesome. Her front teeth were yellow-stained with nicotine.

Three typical juvenile thugs.

Records show that on an average a hundred juvenile gangsters are arrested in London every week, and between them they are responsible for almost exactly half the total of indictable crimes of the City's nine million inhabitants. In every Scotland Yard crime graph the fifteen-year-olds stick out high above every other age group. When you think of a thief you probably have in mind a person about thirty to thirty-five—statistics show the appalling fact that he is more likely to be a child aged fifteen. One robbery in every four is committed by a fourteen- or fifteen-year-old. One stolen car in every five is taken by a 'teen-ager.

These children do not act alone, but in gangs. Some of these 'teen-age gangs number more than a hundred, and there are dozens of smaller mobs. Territory is parceled out as carefully as ever was done in Chicago by the speakeasy barons. A milk-bar on one side of the street can "belong" to one gang, while the soft-drinks bar with the juke-box across the way is in the territory of another gang. Let either side trespass and there may be a battle that may take three or four car-loads of police officers to stop.

Every gang has its team of "brides" or "chicks," who are girls of thirteen to seventeen, painted like Jezebels and captivated by the "glamor" of belonging to a boy gang. These girls often carry their "boy's" initials carved with a knife-blade on arm or leg.

It is as difficult to join one of these gangs as to obtain membership of a good West End club. But—once in—it is almost impossible to get out, except via Borstal or prison. They borrow from the American college fraternity houses the undesirable custom of "initiation ceremonies." A boy will be required to demonstrate—by stealing, fighting or accepting some such challenge as going out deliberately to steal a car or throw a brick at a policeman—that he possesses the required foolhardy viciousness of nature to make him a suitable gang-member. The girls or "brides" pass through initiations that vary according to the particular sadism or prurience of the gang-leaders, but my own information is that no girl who has been accepted as a fully fledged member of any Yobs gang (the word is back-slang, deriving obviously from "Boys") has much virtue left to her.

Very often the parents do not know what is going on. Nor are they always to be blamed one hundred per cent for this ignorance. When yesterday your boy was a lovable child, sensitive to the wishes of his father and mother, it becomes almost impossible to realize that within a short space of months he has become a vicious, irresponsible creature with such dreadful weapons as coshes, home-made stabbing-knives, and knuckle-dusters concealed cunningly in his bedroom, and that he will now lie to you his parents, with utterly bare-faced self-possession. It is hard to think that the gang of "fellows" he spends his time with can be boys with Borstal records, who talk in thievish slang, and of little else but sex and easy money. The signs of dissipation, that we used to know, are no longer present in the child hoodlum of today. He does not touch alcohol, preferring milk-bars and cups of tea in cafés and coffee-stalls.

His dress is, if anything, rather more neat and careful than that of an ordinary, sane youth of similar age. The "spiv" or barrow-boy outfits are demoded now. The zoot-suit, taken from negro musicians, and the "Edwardian era" borrowed from the unsuccessful fashion trend of the West End, are fading, too. The young gangster of today is often from respectable suburban background—surprisingly, too, he is frequently of slightly superior education—and he wears knitted tie, dark suit with pleated hacking slits, fancy waistcoat and thick-soled shoes, often embroidered with leather strips like a Mexican saddle.

They carry weapons to make themselves feel important. They learn that a dozen evil-hearted boys can inspire fear in even three or four grown men, unless such men are specially trained to cope with thugs. Where, yesterday, if a couple of fifteen- or seventeen-year-olds behaved badly in public you would simply smack their silly heads and forget it, the ordinary citizen now runs the risk of being confronted by a dozen or more avenging gang-members, all revoltingly armed.

It is perhaps significant that the Yob Gangs will avenge a slight to their pride more earnestly than anything else. It is in their pride that they are most touchy. They feel their strength like a newly rich woman feels the power of her husband's promotion.

I will give you a shocking example from actual life. It never reached the newspapers. It concerned a decent man named Ted who was an ex-Army non-commissioned officer, and now keeps a small café that a certain Yob gang began to frequent. The police warned him to discourage them, but Ted was sure enough of himself and his sturdy sinews, and thought he understood boys. "They're only going through a phase, Mr. Fabian," he used to tell me. "They'll grow up—it's a kind of cowboys and Indians they are playing. They just carry knives and such stuff to swank with."

But soon the Yobs took advantage, as they always will. They brought young girls in, and they also began spreading obviously stolen property on the white oilcloth table covers. Ted refused to stand for this sort of behavior. He cleared them all out and threatened to tell the police if they came near his café again.

Ted's wife was dead, but he had a daughter, who was just

thirteen years old, a pretty, delicate child and as well-behaved
as you might find anywhere in London. She was terrified of
the Yobs, and her father good-naturedly teased her about this.

A few days after the incident in the café, his daughter
Marigold went off to school in the usual way, but did not
return for tea. When she had not arrived by eight p.m. he
went looking for her. By ten p.m. it occurred to Ted to call
upon the schoolteacher to discover if Marigold had been in
any kind of trouble at school that day. The teacher was at
the cinema, and when she came home she told Ted that his
daughter had not attended school at all that day!

"I think you should go to the police," she said. Ted, hag-
gard with anxiety, was on his way from her house to the police
station, when he met a group of Yobs on the street .corner.
They seemed to be waiting for him, and indeed to be expect-
ing him. The last time he had seen them was the evening he
ordered them out of his café, and their young faces had been
distorted with snarling hatred. Tonight they smiled.

"You look worried, Ted," the leader said politely, and the
father who did not want to quarrel with anybody at that
moment, told them that he was concerned about his daughter
who had not been to school nor had come home that evening.

The Yob leader smiled again. "Pity we aren't friends any
more, Ted, or we might have been able to help you look for
her," he said. A thought came suddenly to Ted. "Do you know
where she is?" He reached out to grasp the young Yob, who
stepped back into the shelter of his fellows. "I haven't seen
her," he said, and he was obviously lying. "But why don't you
have another look at home for her? She's probably home by
now."

There was enough significance in the way the boy spoke,
to make Ted turn towards home instead of to the police station.
The noise of the gang's mirth followed him.

His café was in darkness. He had shut it down that night
while he searched for Marigold. His heart sank with disappointment, for if she had come home she would have turned

the lights on, at least in the living-rooms. But on the doorway
was pinned a notice, made up from letters of the alphabet cut
from newspaper headlines. It said: "Back yard." Ted went
through the house, opened the back door and fell over a
bundle laid across the top step in the darkness. It squirmed
and moaned faintly. It was his little girl, tied up with rope in
a dirty coal sack. Some of her clothing had been pushed into
her mouth and secured there with such vicious tightness that
for several minutes after he removed it she could not move her
jaw. The rest of her clothes were in the sack with her.

As Marigold had been on her usual way to school, a former
schoolmate had stopped her and told of "a puppy crying" in
the boiler-house of a disused property near by. This girl, who
was two years older than Marigold, said she was "afraid to go
down and rescue it, because the place was dark and dirty."

There are few little girls who would be likely to resist such
an appeal. Marigold was no exception. "But I won't be able to
come with you," the girl said, "I shall be late for work." She
had left the school at the end of the previous term. One does
not need to say, presumably, that she was now a member of
the particular bunch of young villains in question.

As Marigold went down the cellar steps, the door between
her and daylight was suddenly closed. She was in complete
darkness, and it was from this blackness that the waiting Yobs
reached her and seized her.

They kept her, bound and blindfold, for nearly fourteen
hours, from morning schooltime until nearly midnight. There
were fully a dozen of them, and they devoted the day to her.
She would not, afterwards, tell even her own father exactly
what had happened during that long day. She was so terrified
that she could not be persuaded even to try to give sensible
evidence against any of them. She had not, of course, seen
their faces.

The only point upon which the police could begin to work,
was the girl who lured her to the cellar. And she—an unusually
depraved and hard-bitten young villain—stuck to her story,

that she had heard the sound of a puppy crying, but had to hurry to work, so had told the first person she saw, who was Marigold.

The police got this girl, a week or two later, as being in need of care or protection, which she undoubtedly was. But, so far, the rest of the Yobs concerned have not been prosecuted, and, whatever punishment they were to receive, it would not be much help to a little girl whom they so terrified that she may never properly recover from her ordeal.

It was such a comparatively small slight—being ordered out of an unimportant café for behaving badly. But the revenge they took was not even straightforward, nor one that might have been understood from the brain of a mischievous boy. They did not smash a window, nor throw in a handful of stink-bombs. What they did was conduct so near to being demoniac, as to be almost out of the class of the ordinary underworld as I have ever known it.

As with so many of the activities of these young gangsters, the deeds they perform and the risks of penalty that they run are out of all sane proportion to the results achieved. The professional criminal has no time for them at all. An ordinary thug —say a racecourse "minder" whose daily job is violence or the threat of violence—would certainly expect £20-£25 for landing a couple of blows with his thick fists at some punter who has perhaps failed to honor his betting obligations. But a 'teen-age gangster, a Yob, will use chains, knives or heavy iron bars with sometimes no more purpose than the satisfaction of terrifying a middle-aged man and his wife who happen to be seated upon a public park bench that the Yobs gang had decided was to be their own customary meeting-place.

When boys belonging to the "Teddy Gang" of Clapham Common conducted themselves in such a hooligan way that another youth was stabbed until he died whilst his arms were held, the prison sentences were nine months and six months. With good behavior—which after all means no more than average behavior in prison—this means six months and four months.

The time soon goes, particularly when you know that the gang-members and the girls are all waiting to hero-worship you as soon as you come out, and when you will in all future years be able to add to your boasting that appalling phrase: "See this knife—I killed a bloke with it!" And everybody will know it to be true.

The Clapham Common affair was briefly this: the leader of the Teddy Gang—an ex-Grammar School boy who distinguished himself and his fellow Yobs by dressing like Edwardian dandies, and who already had a conviction for knocking down an old lady who had not got out of his way—observed that four youths were sprawling on a park seat, and had pulled up another bench to prop their feet on. The gang-leader chose to walk with his girl friend right between these two benches, so that the four youths would have had to stand up to let him pass. The seats were not on a public footpath. There was all the rest of the green common on each side. But that was not good enough for him. He was, perhaps understandably, told to clear off. He did so, and brought back his gang. The four youths were attacked, two gravely injured, and one killed.

When one considers facts like these, it does not seem so unbelievable to hear a story that I was told the other day of a father who discovered that his fourteen-year-old daughter had become a member of such a gang. He refused to allow her to go out in the evenings any more. But a few evenings afterwards he found himself circled by threatening gang-members as he was walking down the street. He lets his daughter out now—he is afraid to stop her.

Whatever kind of home-life can there be, behind such a story, where a child at school can openly defy her own parents? Why do they not go to the police? Because all that would achieve would be a court order sending their child to a remand home as being beyond parental control.

She would still be in the daily company of undesirables, and her parents would be more shamed before their neighbors than they even feel themselves to be today.

The answer to lawless violence should never, of course, be

more lawless violence, or one might feel tempted to advocate the forming of groups of vigilante parents and elder brothers, duly armed with cudgels, to drive these hooligans back into the nursery dream-world of pirates and Red Indians, where they undoubtedly belong mentally!

Part Three

THE GENTLE GRAFTERS

Being a little round-up of characters whose activities undeniably belong to the underworld of London, but who may never be accused of loitering, although they may be said to frequent . . . and whose robberies are seldom violent, but no less painful in result!

Not So Blind

I FIRST MET THE MAN WHO CALLS himself Humphrey Pomfret when I was a uniformed constable. He was begging. It was the year 1922. As I walked down Regent Street I could glimpse his wild, fair hair towering above the crowd that surrounded him. They were mostly women.

He was dressed in military hospital blue with scarlet tie and white shirt. He was selling boot-laces and match-boxes—a pitifully common occupation in those days among crippled ex-heroes of the Somme and Marne. His handsome face was pale.

The women were stuffing his pockets with silver and ten-shilling notes—which was big money then. A little placard, no bigger than a library book, hung upon his back and chest:

"IT IS SPRING—AND I AM BLIND."

Several women were openly weeping into little sopping handkerchiefs.

Then I saw his medals. He had the Croix de Guerre, the Mons Star, General Service Medal and the Military Cross—in that order! Any soldier will tell you why I promptly arrested him.

The crowd of women nearly lynched me as I led him away. But at the old Vine Street (now West End Central) police station, he admitted he had never been in the army.

He was only partly blind. And that, I discovered, had not been caused by mustard gas on the Somme, but by an explosion in a Clerkenwell basement kitchen, when he was heating nitric and sulphuric acids in a frying pan, and adding glycerine from a scent spray. He was trying to make safe-breaker's nitroglycerine. He succeeded! It cost him seventy-five per cent of his normal eyesight.

For wearing medals and uniform unlawfully, he was fined.

Today the man who calls himself Pomfret has one eye completely restored. But he still pretends to be blind. It makes it easier for him to swindle his victims when he sells them antiques, jewelry, furs and Oriental rugs.

You may—if you are rich and foolish—have in your home today some treasured *objet d'art* you bought from Humphrey Pomfret. You will have paid a small fortune for it. It will be worth about £2.

He puts out small advertisements. Whatever he offers for sale—antique diamond brooch, genuine Persian rug, Rembrandt painting—when you ring the tinkly doorbell of his flat, he will greet you with charming apologies.

"I am so sorry—an American positively bustled in and purchased it—for cash, would you believe it? But do come in and have a little refreshment—a glass of sherry, or perhaps China tea?"

These days, Humphrey Pomfret's hair is grey, but still curly. His face is still handsome. His dark glasses still make him poignant. He seems obviously blind. But he leads the way unfalteringly about his beautiful apartment, with only a light touch upon wall, door or table-edge for guidance.

"See! My tropical fish are lively today! Such beautiful colors—jewels of the sea, indeed! Ah!"—he pauses in front of an antique, gilt-framed painting, and switches on a tiny illumination for it—"at this time of an afternoon my El Greco is in shadow."

As you look at the painting, he says, half to himself: "To me, it is always in shadow, these days—but one's mind's eye does not quickly forget such grace—such lively brushwork!"

He shows his treasures, fondles them blindly. You sit, sipping your Vino de Pasto, and would be a hard mortal not to feel deeply moved. . . .

"Let me see—it was my Feraghan rug you came to buy? Such a pity—I feel from your voice that you, too, find happiness in beauty. Tell me"—he hesitates—"would one of my Kashmiri rugs appeal to you?" He waves his long fingers towards the rug draped over the white piano. It is silk. A genuine silk Kashmere is the mink of the rug world.

"One must be so careful in buying rugs." He shows you the rug and gives you a gentle lecture on the pitfalls of antique rug-buying.

"Many are fakes—mercerized cotton, woven on power-looms, and not by hand! I have even detected rugs where the genuine, hand-tied Ghiordes knot is faked by pulling loops of unknotted yarn through a base resembling the true warp."

His hands flutter over the rug. "Always examine the back of a rug, eh? It is the only way to tell the genuine article—particularly with these flat-stitch Kashmiri. That mellow sheen—they sometimes fake it by washing the rug in bleach to soften the harsh colors, then make a false lustre with hot irons and glycerine!"

He shakes his head sadly. "Ah, but I think the genuine connoisseur can always tell—even when he is nearly blind, as I am. See, my dear fellow—spit upon the rug, so! Rub the nap, and smell it. If it smells bleachy, it is a fake. But that unmis-

takably goaty smell can surely mean only the genuine thing,
eh?" (Actually it means that Mr. Pomfret was busy before
you arrived, rubbing Stilton cheese into that particular corner
of the fake rug he will shortly permit you to pay him £300
for!)

Perhaps it is an emerald brooch, or sapphire bracelet—
"Belonged to one of the ladies of the Gaiety chorus, I believe!"
The "emerald" will be a thin slice of garnet (which passes all
the hardness tests of an emerald), fused to a piece of green
glass. And the beautiful deep-blue sapphire will be two slices
of cheap, pale sapphire, stuck together with translucent blue
cement, and known to the jewel trade as a "doublet."

The only way you can detect these fakes is to take the
stones from their settings and stand them on edge in water.
But you are not likely to do that—not while the charming,
pathetic Mr. Pomfret is telling you every other known test of
a fake emerald or sapphire, from showing you how to use a
jeweler's glass and looked for chipped edges and scratches
(which won't be there), to the technique of a Hatton Garden
dichroscope, which shows up the spectrum of a stone on
elaborate enlarging screens. You are not likely to have a
dichroscope in your car, and Mr. Pomfret knows it.

His trick is to give a lecture on the Art of Spotting a Fake,
then—with a disarming reminder that he is himself almost
blind—leave it to you to be the judge. It seldom fails. If you
want to buy his El Greco, he will say: "Alas! There are many
forgeries among El Grecos. Before I could think of discussing
a price for this picture, I would want you to consult an
expert."

He unhooks it lovingly, escorts you into a hired limousine
—my driving days are over, my dear fellow!"—and you go to
one of the reputable galleries around Old Bond Street.

Mr. Pomfret stays in the car, a tall, poignant elderly gentleman, while you are trusted to remove the El Greco from the
limousine, and pay the art expert a spot consultation fee.

You will learn that the picture is genuine and that it is

worth £3,000. You return with it to the car and offer Mr. Pomfret £2,000.

He is disappointed. "Really? I would have supposed—perhaps £3,000? But you say it is valued at £2,000—ah, well." He nods, resignedly.

You give him your check for £2,000. You feel rather a cad.

But sensitive Mr. Pomfret cannot endure to think of a horrid blank space on the wall of his beautiful apartment. "Allow me two days, my dear fellow, to find another picture." He adds, delicately, that it will take two days to clear your check.

You see his point. But, while you hesitate, Mr. Pomfret produces his gold fountain pen. "Honor me by signing your name on the back of the canvas, and there shall be no doubt then, in either of our minds, that the sale has been completed, and my El Greco is now your property."

You sign. Two days later you call to collect your painting. This time, you are not invited beyond the hallway. Mr. Pomfret is curt.

"I am informed," he says loftily, "that the value of the El Greco is nearer £3,000 than £2,000, sir! Nevertheless, I shall honor our bargain."

He gives you the painting. Your signature is still on the back of the canvas. He shows you out, coldly.

When you get home, it may be months or years before an expert tells you the painting is a fake, worth about £60. Even if it is only twenty-four hours before you learn the truth, it will be too late. Mr. Pomfret has departed. He did not want you past the hallway because his furniture was in the removing van!

How did he do it? A second canvas was stuck to the back of the genuine El Greco, both in the one frame. It was his back canvas you put your signature upon with Mr. Pomfret's gold fountain pen. Well, he warned you there were many El Greco forgeries about!

I could tell you a similar story about antique furniture. Yes, that can be faked too—even with the worm-holes in it. Have you ever seen a worm-hole-making machine at work? I have. It's a fine drill which puts the holes just where you want them —and just like the worm makes them.

In the art-treasure game there are a lot of crooks about. *and* a lot of mugs! Mr. Pomfret knows.

Lɪᴛᴛʟᴇ ᴅᴇɴɪꜱᴇ ʟᴏᴏᴋꜱ ꜱᴍᴀʀᴛ, ᴀᴅᴠᴇɴᴛᴜʀᴏᴜꜱ, and rather expensive. She has an air about her, and a whiff of good perfume.

I saw her first, and raised my newspaper to hide my face as she came into the cocktail bar.

Her black Persian lamb coat had been shaped for no other waist than hers and she carried a little matching muff. Also a bundle of beautifully wrapped shopping packages.

"A White Lady, please," she said, and balanced her heap of costly looking bundles upon the empty stool beside her.

In no time at all the top package—with wrapping paper of Garrards, the Court jewelers, in Albemarle Street—had fallen to the floor. The sporty-looking, prosperous chap who had been gulping his second large Scotch picked it up.

"Cigarette?"

"Well—thank you." She accepted one, "I'm really dying

for a cigarette." She dipped a gloved hand into her little accessory-bag and located a ten-shilling note to pay for her drink.

'Absolutely my last," she laughed. "I've been on a shopping spree—had to choose between a drink, cigarettes, or a taxi to Sloane Square. The drink won, and now I think I shall buy some cigarettes, and take a bus home."

The sporty-looking chap wanted to buy her some cigarettes but she would not allow it. Nor would she let him pay for her drink. But when he said upon his honor that he was heading toward Sloane Square that very instant, she consented to share his taxi.

I did not feel that it was up to me to interfere. At Scotland Yard the photograph, full-face and profile, fingerprints and fascinating dossier upon Little Denise are all waiting. If the sporty-looking man wished to go to the Yard next day and run his eye through the photos, he could pick out and accuse Little Denise without any help from me.

But I don't suppose he ever did go to the police. He wouldn't want his wife to know. And the Mayfair Girls seldom appear before the magistrates.

They are not street-girls. They would slap your face for the suggestion, would Little Denise (whose real name I understand to be Agnes), or demure little Daisy, or red-haired Thelma who looks like Rita Hayworth, and wears country tweeds by Lachasse, millinery by Vernier (her dad is a french-polisher on the Walworth Road).

They do not even get their victims into an embarrassing situation, then rip their blouses and threaten to scream for help unless he pays up promptly. The nearest their victim—whom we can call Mr. Eager—gets to a kiss is when his money kisses him good-bye!

In that taxi towards Sloane Square, Little Denise would have handled hearty Mr. Eager with smooth artistry. Mr. Eager may perhaps be hopeful of taking her to dine and dance, that night.

"Then I must change from this dusty old outfit," declares Denise, and crinkles her adorable nose at her flawless garb. "I'll give you a drink at my flat, while I have a quick bath and change."

In the taxi, she says: "Stop at Fortnum and Mason's please. They will actually let me have three bottles of real Scotch, and I need some more vermouth and bitters, and things."

Ah—but—she has no money with her. She spent it all, shopping . . . remember?

She borrows a couple of fivers. "Keep an eye on my parcels —they're rather valuable," she says. "The commissionaire will bring the bottles out to the taxi for me."

She leaves Mr. Eager to wait with all those beautiful parcels in the taxi, while she disappears into Fortnum and Masons. She goes in at the door at the corner of Jermyn Street and leaves quickly by the Piccadilly entrance.

Mr. Eager waits and waits. The taxi-meter ticks and ticks. The packages? Well, they're any sort of rubbish, wrapped in parcel-paper stamped with Old Bond Street, the Burlington Arcade, etc.

Little Denise can wrap nifty parcels. She used to be a shop-girl.

Demure little Daisy takes longer, with her own particular piracy. She takes a bigger risk, and gets a bigger reward.

She looks a bit lonesome, and has the air of a nice young widow. She knows a thousand innocent-seeming ways to make you speak to her. When you do, she will answer shyly. She does not encourage human wolves and boudoir-lizards. Daisy seeks the solid, comfortable married men who come to London on a few days' business trip.

She likes to be taken to a tearoom, where she coos over squashy cream-cakes and China tea. She removes her little gloves, and Mr. Fairleigh-Eager observes the wedding ring and beautiful 1¼-carat diamond solitaire engagement ring, in perfect quiet taste.

She lowers her eyes. "I'm separated from my husband," she

says, and explains that she was given custody of the toddler, who is now at a good residential nursery school.

She recounts a few shuddering examples of her husband's cruelties, and Mr. Fairleigh-Eager puts his hand sympathetically upon hers. She does not remove it.

Perhaps Miss Daisy will say that she is on a lonesome holiday, or has just lost her job. They meet two or three times.

She pauses at a jeweler's window. "Why, there's a ring like mine, and only £250!" she says. This upsets her, for she had always understood her own ring—her only bit of jewelry—was worth about £400.

The jeweler squints at Daisy's ring, and shakes his head. "Not worth more than £250, madam," he says. "You'd be lucky to get £150 for it, from a dealer."

They go to lunch. They go to dinner. . . . Sooner or later, Daisy breaks the news that she must pay little Jennifer's fees at the residential nursery school, or the child will be flung out. Daisy needs a loan of £80 to £100 until the end of the month, or whenever she usually gets her quarterly separation allowance check from her husband's solicitors.

Mr. Fairleigh-Eager hesitates unhappily. And Daisy blushes (you may do this by holding your breath and compressing your diaphragm in a certain way. Any good actor of the old school can show you).

"Of course, you don't know me very well . . . but I've nobody else in the world . . ." she is playing frantically with her engagement ring, and suddenly she remembers it, and smiles. "But how silly of me—here, you must have this as a security!"

Mr. Fairleigh-Eager heard the jeweler put its value at £150. It seems a pity to spoil this promising, clandestine little romance for a loan with such good security. That will be the last he sees of his money. And of Daisy.

The ring? It was an American diamothyst, the new "laboratory" diamond that will deceive any but an expert, and is worth exactly one-thirtieth of an ordinary diamond in market value.

Why didn't the jeweler spot it for a fake? Because he never saw it. The ring the jeweler examined was a genuine diamond. Daisy just slipped the genuine ring into her glove, and from that moment on wore the imitation.

It's a good business, selling diamothyst rings at three thousand per cent profit. Especially for an attractive girl!

"**P**UT THESE PAPERS IN THE HOTEL SAFE for me, please!" said the tall and soldierly gentleman in the expensive tweeds. "They're rather valuable."

The big envelope rustled and crackled impressively. The hotel manager bowed. "Pleasure, Colonel."

"And are there any letters for me?"

There were. Half a dozen important-looking envelopes, some with crests, some with seals. The Colonel took them.

Later, when the guests had retired to bed, a cleaner discovered a batch of papers in a deep armchair in one of the lounges. They were income-tax forms and receipts, for many thousands of pounds. They bore the name of the Colonel. Next morning they were returned to him by the manager.

The Colonel thrust them into his pocket. "Oh, thanks—blasted income tax," he said. The manager was very respectful by this time.

That afternoon, as the waiter was almost falling over the

little coffee tables to ensure that the wealthy Colonel was not kept waiting for the expensive cigars he had just ordered, a quiet man in a lounge-suit came into the room and gazed around it with practiced care. Nobody noticed him.

His glance fell upon the soldierly-looking gentleman. He smiled sadly and moved over to him.

"Pack your bags, Jim," he murmured almost affectionately, "and pay your bill with good money—and don't take any silver spoons or spare towels with you, my boy. And if you're not out of this hotel within fifteen minutes . . ."

The Colonel went pale. But it was not with indignation. He did not argue. Before the fifteen minutes he had left the Splendide Hotel for ever.

And that was just another incident in the day's routine of ex-Detective-Inspector Jock McBogey, who is house detective —he calls it "security superintendent"—at one of London's most exclusive hotels. He had recognized the soldierly gentleman as an oft-convicted confidence trickster.

"It's the easiest trick in the world to tinker with your income-tax papers and make 'em look as if you're a millionaire," he says. "And the same with bank-books."

The big hotels of London are in a state of daily—and nightly—siege by the tricksters and thieves of the underworld, and their women. The more exclusive and snooty an hotel, the more will villians strive to get inside it, where pickings are rich.

Nearly every West End hotel has its own "Millionaires' Row"—entire floors of expensive suites where the world's wealthiest people can live for months and years, paying rents up to £85 a week, not including meals!

The job of keeping screwsmen out of these suites is one duty of the hotel detective. For the Metropolitan policeman and the Yard's patrol cars can't prowl the carpeted, quiet corridors, glittering restaurants, cocktail bars, grill rooms, tea rooms and banqueting halls, of London's big hotels, even though richer loot exists inside than in Aladdin's cave!

So the hotels snap up ex-Yard men, at comfortable salaries
—£500 to £1,200 on top of their police pensions—to become
hotel detectives, privileged to enjoy all meals at the hotel,
keep their own bedrooms and offices. They have their own
staffs of two to five ex-Metropolitan C.I.D. men under them.
Here's a few of them—all ex-colleagues of mine at Scotland
Yard: Detective-Inspector Fred Elliott at the Dorchester,
Inspector Jenkins at the Savoy, Detective-Inspector Smart at
Grosvenor House, Detective-Inspector Cecil Warner at the
Regent Palace, Detective-Sergeant Gray at the Hyde Park
Hotel, Detective-Sergeant Jean Nicholls at the Cumberland. . . .

Inside an hotel like the Dorchester is a vast fortune in
silverware, linen, cutlery and crockery. Any of the top dozen
London hotels could easily pay the Prime Minister's salary
from what it loses each week by "souvenir hunters"—as amateur thieves are politely called.

Towels, ash-trays, wall-mirrors, drinking-glasses by the
hundred, paintings from the walls, bedside lamps, silk bed-
covers, sheets, blankets—even corridor carpets rolled up and
smuggled away!

"We put it on the bill," explains McBogey. "That usually
does the trick."

Petty thieving is one of the least problems of the hotel
detective. Almost any quiet afternoon at Scotland Yard, you
may observe ex-colleagues busily turning over the method-
index files in the Modus Operandi Room, to see if the boys
have dreamed up any bright new techniques for hotel swindles.
They learn the Rogues' Gallery Portraits almost by heart. The
French Sûreté and American F.B.I. keep them constantly
posted with dossiers and photos of thieves in transit, persons
wanted, etc.

You might be horrified how much a hotel detective can get
to know about you, without asking you a single question.
There is even a private code used between hotels in pasting
labels upon luggage. Many of the big continental hotels use
it. I dare not disclose it—except that if the label is upside

down, it means a rotten tipper! If your luggage is expensive, but your shaving brush, razor and underwear are cheap, the hotel detective staff is likely to keep you under wary, invisible scrutiny.

The guests who bring cockroaches in matchboxes, and pretend to discover them in beds or food, or baby rats in their spare shoes, and threaten to sue for damages, are old stuff to McBogey. So is the thief, dressed as a mechanic, who arrives early in the morning at the hotel garage, with a chit "to collect the magneto and batteries from Vauxhall AB 1234."

Drunks are easy. McBogey and his assistants can whisk a troublesome drunk from bar or lounge, without any guest noticing what has happened. They each seize his arm above the elbow, twist their fingers around the bottom of his jacket-sleeves, and talk to him with wide, easy smiles, effectively drowning his mumbling protests, as they stroll to a taxi, like three gentlemen in happy conversation.

Women are the worst problem. A young lady may book a room, or sit in the lounge for coffee. She smiles at a man. Is he an acquaintance? He might even be her husband, with whom she is trying to patch up a quarrel. Or it may be that immorality has come to the hotel. A wrong word, a hasty decision, and the hotel is due for a savage legal action, with heavy damages.

Yet it is a serious offense for an hotel-keeper to "allow persons to congregate for immoral purposes," and one of the most amazing compliments to the diplomatic efficiency of London's hotel detectives is that a prosecution under this clause is almost unknown in the Metropolis.

"Anyone can spot a genuine honeymoon couple," says McBogey. "They're no problem. But the hardened sinner who signs 'Mr. and Mrs. Smith' with a flourish, is difficult. Even so, you can tell them, when they come to the reception clerk and discuss type of room, price, with bath or lounge, etc. A real husband and wife exchange little glances, a kind of private telegraphy. And when they get to their room, they want to know about things like hot-water bottles, the valet service, how long the laundry takes. But the sinner and his week-end girl, when they get to their room, ring down for drinks! Also, their luggage is often of contrasting quality—his perhaps of pigskin, and hers a simple fibre suitcase."

The name of a good hotel must not appear too often in the divorce news. But every hotel gets caught occasionally. Then the house charge is five guineas for making chambermaids, waitresses, etc., available for questioning by private inquiry agents.

When you go to your hotel room and snip down the little catch that is fixed to the inside door lock, the chambermaid cannot get in. But McBogey can. He carries a special key, and there is a secret flange inside the lock, that operates the "privacy catch" on the door, when McBogey turns his key in reverse. If he catches you red-handed in sin, he will not make a scene. He will tell you that your "custom is no longer required." And he will take a penetrating look at your face, with his trained policeman's eye.

You won't get into that hotel again. Nor, under the same name, in any hotel of the combine. They will always "regret there is no room available." For the hotel detectives, guardians of fabulous fortunes in furs, jewels—and morals—have a private black-list of their own. It would be worth much to a blackmailer. But no blackmailer will ever see it. Blackmailers rate even lower, with Jock McBogey, than "honeymooners without marriage lines," as he delicately calls them!

MY FRIEND CARADOC HAS FOR TWENTY-FIVE years been a police officer in the Welsh hills. He married a country girl, and they were both very good to me when I went up to Wales once with the Murder Bag.

Recently Caradoc retired. He'd had a good career, though a bit quiet. He was red-hot on sheep-stealing, drunks and speed offenses of the big, laden trucks that thundered through the lonely Welsh mountain-passes.

"I want to keep a pub in London," he told me, in his liltingly musical voice. "My wife has set her heart upon it, and we've saved nearly £800."

"With £800 and your testimonials you can probably get a tenancy in a London pub," I said, "but you should be warned, Caradoc."

He lifted his bushy, gray-streaked eyebrows, and his

countryman's eyes were as clear as a child's. "Warned, man? Warned about what?"

I said: "There are 7,774 public houses in London, and over a quarter of a million pounds in cash goes jingling across their bar-counters every night.

"If there's only one dishonest barmaid in London," I said, "you can be sure that she'll come to you for a job, Caradoc. If there's only one villainous cellarman on the Employment Agency cards, he'll come to your public house, my lad! And they'll skin you alive, and you'll never know what hit you!"

It was obvious that Caradoc felt a little hurt. "I'm a policeman, man—I've come up against a crook or two in my time, you know—even if I was never at your Scotland Yard," he said. But he was too good-natured to take offense, and too well trained a policeman to miss the chance of learning something. So he added, after a moment: "What sort of tricks would they be up to, now?"

I took Caradoc and his wife to meet my friend Barney, who keeps a public house in the depths of Soho's jungle. There are not many fools among London's publicans. Most of them have a peeled eye for a sharp trick. But Barney is the prince of them all. He is as quick as Buffalo Bill.

We walked into his pub just before eleven a.m. opening time. The barmaid had just taken off her hat and coat, and the cellarman was rinsing water through the pumps.

"Welcome to you, Mr. Fabian," said Barney affably. "You'll excuse me a minute, because this barmaid is fresh from the agency this morning. I shall have to put her into the right way of a few matters."

We had a look at the new barmaid. Her name was Freda, and she was dark, pert, with vindictive little wrinkles around her painted mouth. She looked tough, young and sly. But she she could smile nicely when she wanted to, and was obviously going to be popular with the customers, particularly after their third or fourth drink.

"Now, my dear," said Barney, "have you brought your

cards, and your identity card? Left them at your last job, did you? Ah, well, we can get them tomorrow, can't we?" He threw a quick glance at me, and I knew what he meant. Freda obviously needed watching.

She combed her black hair, and put her handbag under the counter, still open, with the comb sticking out.

Barney picked up the handbag and placed it on the second shelf up in front of the bar mirror. To reach it now, Freda would need to stretch to her full height.

"And if you'll just empty all your cash from your pockets into it, my dear," said Barney, "as is the rule of all well-conducted public houses in this city, we shall expect no confusion between my petty cash and your bus money when we come to checking-up time, shall we?"

Freda pouted and gave him an old-fashioned look. But Barney was within his rights, and she knew it.

To the cellarman, Barney called: "When you've put a barrel on and pulled a glass that's fit to drink yourself, Sam, then drink it and good health to you. But don't pull your tests into that big white jug, there's a good boy—or it might get sold by mistake while you're helping Freda in the rush-hour!"

Barney lifted a chair and came to sit with us. I told him what Caradoc and his wife had in mind to do, and he was at once sympathetic.

"You'll find your staff are fairly easy if you keep a bit of an eye on 'em," he said. "It's some of the casual bar staff that has to be watched a bit." He lowered his voice. "That girl, for instance—she's a 'floater'—never keeps a job more than a few days. Some like her are honest, and some just scheme to fiddle twenty to thirty pounds in four or five day's work, then take a week's pay for notice when you begin to suspect something—and off to the next job!"

"Are there a lot of them, man?" said Caradoc thoughtfully.

Barney shrugged. "Well, you have to remember that each time a 'floater' moves on, she leaves a vacancy behind her, for another 'floater' to fill. Still," he said, "if you make sure she has no money in her pockets when she goes behind the bar, and that her purse is well in sight all the time, then all you have to do is see the dirty water is drained from the sink before you check the night's takings—it's wonderful how often a few half-crowns get dropped 'by accident' into the sink-water!

"And often there's a pound note stuck under the soap," said Barney, "or inside the barmaid's cigarette packet—or a packet she sells across the counter to a friend, or tucked in her shoe, or rolled up under her hair-slide, or hid behind the radiator-pipe for a croney to pick up, or left inside an empty match-box in the toilet, or"—he glanced doubtfully at Freda—"when they wear low dresses like that, I must say it makes things a bit difficult, but you just have to concentrate on hope eternal, that's all!"

Caradoc did not understand the last remark, but he was puzzled anyway. "Surely you can tell when you check the cash-register, how much money is missing?"

Barney gave a long-suffering smile. "If you pour a quart bottle smartly, with a nice lively 'top' on it, sir—you can easy get five half-pint glasses full. That doesn't make arithmetic, but it makes a profit.

"If you wedge a shilling into the bottom of the measuring-tot, then one whisky, gin and rum out of every six sold, belongs to the barmaid. It's never difficult to short-change a customer when he's had a drink or two—give him change for ten bob instead of a pound, or bang the coins down hard on the counter while he's talking hard, and flick a couple of bob away from the heap. Most drinkers get so busy blathering, they don't seem to know nor care if they get their correct change!

"Of course," said Barney, "if the landlord's in it, too, he'll fix a bit of celluloid into the 'optic pouring measure' on all the spirit bottles, and save himself one bottle in every twelve sold.

"As for checking the cash-register," said Barney, "excuse me a minute!" He sauntered to the bar, where Freda was serving a large port-and-brandy to a gentleman with a head-ache. Freda had tossed the bar-cloth carelessly across the cash-register while she left her hands free to ring up the amount.

Barney quietly removed the cloth. "If you do that, dear," he said steadily, "the customer can't see how much you ring up, because the cloth is obscuring the cash-register—and it's just as well in this case, dear, because it only shows sixpence instead of five and sixpence. I expect that five-shilling key didn't hit properly, dear." Freda blushed.

"Not that the customer usually bothers," said Barney as he came back to our table. "But I do. The sort of cash-register you must avoid, is the one where you write with a bit of pencil in a space on a roll of paper, and when you open the cash-drawer the paper jerks up another space."

"Why, there's one of them in our village shop," said Caradoc suddenly, "and man, I always thought it must be foolproof!"

Barney smiled sadly. "Well, if you write down six in the pence column, when it should be in the shilling column, and do this five or six times daily, you aren't doing so badly. If the boss checks the till, he must wait until he can take the whole paper roll out, and wind it back."

"I see," said Caradoc, and it seemed that his country cheeks had gone a little paler.

"Mind you," said Barney, "the things that a thieving cellar-man can do to you shouldn't happen to one's mother-in-law. In a big pub, with five or six barmaids and a day's turnover of £200, every two-gallon bucket of water's worth two or three quid to a cellarman with a pal upstairs. Then there's the customers themselves . . ."

"The customers?" Caradoc swallowed with difficulty.

"Heavens, yes," said Barney, "some of the customers do as much fiddling as ever gets done behind the bar, believe me!"

"I will believe you," said Caradoc earnestly, "but tell me about it!"

"For a start, you've got to keep your eyes peeled for

betting-slips," said Barney, "and if you don't they can take your license away. Every time a couple of sporty girls come in for a gin-and-lime, you must take care you don't get done for 'allowing persons to congregate for immoral purposes'—and you've had it off properly if either of 'em is under eighteen— as if an honest man can tell, with all this pancake make-up stuff!"

Caradoc loosened his tie. "Go on, man," he said. Barney went on.

"The number of commercial travelers who pull out wallets stuffed with credentials and want checks cashing, and leave their cars in your garage as security until next day when the banks open," said Barney, "and next day the police turn up, looking for stolen car number so-and-so, and it's in your blinkin' garage!"

He sipped his cup of tea. "It isn't just cashing dud checks," he said, "which nobody but a proper mug would do. But when a customer complains he gave a pound note and only has change for ten shillings, and pulls out four or five quid fresh from the bank, to prove the last quid in the till has a matching serial number, what can you do? You know he must have an accomplice who slipped the quid in the round before, but if they both pretend they're strangers, where are you?"

"Stung," I said, and Barney nodded. "Stung is right, Mr. Fabian. You'll get chaps who'll order a pint of beer, gulp more than half of it, then say indignantly that the stuff's got grease floating on it. Of course it has—an' them with a halibut liver oil capsule in their teeth, that they nip as they splutter a bit of beer back into the tankard!"

"Yes, it's a lively game, is the publican's trade in London," said Barney. "I'm not saying it's worse nor better than in the provinces, but when I retire, I shall take a little public house somewhere among the Welsh mountains, where the trade's mostly beer, and you can draw it yourself, and have one with the boys, and join in the singing on Saturday nights!"

"That mightn't be a bad idea, man," said Caradoc, and scratched his chin thoughtfully. . . .

Part Four

TALES OF DARKNESS

The Blitz Site Murder

THE WEEDS THAT HAD GROWN UP IN THE blitz site were dead now. The woman who lay among them was dead too, but more recently. Blood from her crushed forehead still shone wet.

The murderer had gone, abandoning his death weapon. When he had stooped to grope for the fatal hammer, weeds hid it. So he hurried away, sure of not being seen along that empty midnight Manchester Street. And as he stepped across the dead woman, his neat grey trousers brushed the willowherb weeds. The murderer strode on to his hostel smirking. He felt it was a murder well done. He did not know that an invisible Judas now walked with him, waiting to betray.

Two children found the woman's body next day. They were walking home from early Mass, and adventured off Deansgate in neatly polished Sabbath shoes to cross the bare patch that war-bombs had cleared behind Northcliffe House.

"Look, Arthur!" shrilled little Terry Cordner, "a lady's legs!"

Dark blood dappled the weeds. Police hurried from the city's C.I.D. headquarters in Bootle Street across the way.

"Dead about six hours," said the surgeon. "Probably midnight."

Chief Detective-Inspector Daniel Timpany searched among the woman's numerous clothes. On her were two coats, two frocks. On each sprawled leg, two lisle stockings. Her body was her wardrobe, marking her to Timpany as a woman of the lodging-houses and night cafés. A delicacy of face was still traceable. Greyness had crept into her auburn hair. Her hand-bag held two £1 notes and an identity card: Olive Balchin, Blythsford Road, Birmingham.

Five strides from the body, Timpany picked up a hammer, stuck among the weeds by skeins of blood.

At Bootle Street Police H.Q., his C.I.D. chief, Superinten-dent William Page, considered the murder weapon. Page, big and soft-spoken, turned the hammer thoughtfully. "That's no hammer for knocking nails in—look at the ends of it—both convex—like big revolver bullets. It's a tradesman's hammer." He handed it to a subordinate. "Find what craftsman's tool it is."

The report came quickly: "Used by leather-beaters, sir. Gold-beaters, less frequently. Weighs four pounds, twelve-inch handle."

"Send a photo of it to the newspapers," said Page. He dispatched detectives to discover if anything had been seen or heard that night among the shut shops and empty offices of Deansgate.

One man had seen something. Mr. Norman Mercer, land-lord of the "Dog and Partridge," taking his dog for a brief midnight stroll down Deansgate: "I saw a man and woman, talking loudly, near the blitz site. She wore a blue coat with big pearl buttons. His hair was dark, well-greased." Olive Balchin's outer coat was blue with big pearl buttons!

Most honest folk in Manchester are at home by midnight. Only the night buses run. Hotels switch out foyer lights, leave just a pilot-bulb for the night-porter. Detectives visited hotels, lodging-houses, hostels, cafés, sandwich-stalls, taxis, night-bus conductors. . . .

At the Queen's Café, behind Deansgate, a tired waitress remembered a man with dark greased hair and two women. She was shown Olive Balchin's death-photo and went pale. "That was one of them!"

But of the man with dark, greased hair there was no further clue. Until Monday morning. Then, fumbling nervously at his dark cap, came Mr. Edward McDonald. He held a copy of a daily newspaper. "This photo of a hammer—I sold that hammer on Saturday night!"

Mr. McDonald had a small broker-shop near Ardwick. "For three and sixpence," he said, "I sold it to this chap. I asked him what he wanted a hammer like that for, at six o'clock of a Saturday night."

The police lifted slow, interested eyebrows. "What did he say?"

"He said: 'I want this hammer for general purposes.' I told him: 'It won't be much use for knocking nails and things. But he just picked it up and tested it in his hand then said: 'It will suit my purpose,' and he smiled a bit queerly."

Mr. McDonald had been disturbed by the man. So he had remembered him, and could give a fair description. Police now started seeking a man with fair hair brushed back, tight-compressed mouth with taut, crumpled lines around it. A floppy white collar, grey suit, blue pullover. Average build.

After five days' search, detectives entered a lodging-house within a mile of the murder. "Anybody of this description?"

The hostel-keeper considered. "Funny thing," he said. "Chap like that's been here nearly a week, and hardly ever left his room!"

The detectives went up to the small, dreary room. A man lay sleeping. Grey suit and blue pullover lay on a wooden chair beside him.

"Why, hullo, Rowland!" said Detective-Inspector Stainton softly, as he woke him. "Better come with us!"

They knew the man as Walter Graham Rowland, aged thirty-eight, with a criminal record. At nineteen, charged with attempted murder of a girl, served three years Borstal for grievous bodily harm. Two years after release, murdered his two-year-old daughter, sentenced to death but reprieved. From Parkhurst Prison, after nine years, Rowland volunteered for the Army, had been demobbed into freedom only six months ago.

"Is it about that Balchin woman?" asked Rowland, sitting up sleepily. Then, as he realized what he had said, his mouth shut into its customary clamped suspicious trap.

From a dinner-party, Superintendent Page hurried to the bare police office where Rowland sat sipping tea, untroubled.

"I am innocent," said Rowland. "All you have against me is my past record. I can prove an alibi."

Two people said they had seen Rowland in a Stockport tavern eight miles away from the Queen's Café, within half an hour of the time stated in the waitress's evidence. He had been there most of the evening, they said. How could he buy a hammer in Manchester?

The evidence conflicted. Each faction of witnesses grew more confused, more heated and less certain. Manchester police officials hesitated. There were no fingerprints on the hammer.

"Send his clothes to the police laboratories," ordered Superintendent Page.

Next afternoon came the scientific report. "Blood speck on trouser turn-ups, too slight for group identification. Brick-dust, cement-dust, charcoal, clinker and withered leaf tissue (genus: *Polygonum*, commonly, willow-herb weed or knot weed). Hair on Rowland's jacket matches hair of dead woman, red with henna traces, beginning to turn grey."

"Analyze the blitz-site rubble!" said Page. The laboratory

A friendly chat with Roy Birchenough at his club

Frisco buys me a drink, so I ring up—"No Sale"

This is "Ackey" who has had a barrow for as long as I can remember

Having a cup of coffee with some of my colored friends

Scotland Yard by night, the G.H.Q. of a ceaseless battle
waged against London's underworld of crime and vice

Beneath the lights of the Embankment, and with Big Ben in the
background, Old Father Thames flows slowly towards the sea

With fountains playing, Trafalgar Square is the most famous spot in the world.
In the background is St. Martin-in-the-Fields, the crypt of which never closes

Piccadilly Circus, where the pulsing heart of London is most truly felt

The lights of Leicester Square act as a magnet to Londoners and visitors from overseas

report was identical: "brick-dust, cement-dust, charcoal, clinker and withered willow-herb weed."

The dead, unheeded flowers of a city blitz-site had, it seemed, left their Judas-kiss upon the hem of a murderer's garment!

Seven weeks later, Walter Graham Rowland walked tight-lipped into the condemned cell of Strangeways Prison. Snow whirled and fell upon the bleak yard outside. He made towards the wall. His signature, where he had scratched it in 1934, was still faintly there. Slowly, with the edge of his thumb-nail, Rowland scratched an amendment:

"ALSO . . . DECEMBER 16, 1946."

He looked around the narrow room. The two warders watched him. Rowland's tight lips uncoiled in a strange, fiercely proud smile.

"There's nobody else but me—ever—walked into this room twice!" he said.

Two months later he was hanged. And it was to this self-same murder that John David Ware confessed, and was officially judged to be telling an untruth, shortly before Rowland was executed. Years afterward, Ware criminally attacked a woman, and is today in Broadmoor.

Was his "confession" truth or an insane fantasy? If it were correct that Rowland did not kill Olive Balchin, it would be the first time in my experience that a man had been wrongly hanged under British law. My own belief is that Ware, who had an insane urge concerning the "hitting of women on the head"—to use his own words—entangled himself in dream fantasy with Olive Balchin's murder, just as an adolescent girl will sometimes make accusations of indecent assault that are entirely without truthful foundation.

MARY CLARKE WAS AFRAID OF THE NEW lodger's razor, long before she could have known he was going to cut her throat with it. When he began to shave she had to hurry from his room and wait trembling in the corridor.

The lodger had come recently to Mrs. Pannell's apartment house at No. 14 Brownlow Street, which is just behind the benign towers of Liverpool Royal Infirmary. Mrs. Pannell put him in the ground-floor back room, relieved to learn that he required no meals, and even more relieved when he paid his ten shillings rent promptly at the end of the first week.

The lodger was forty-eight years old, had a craggy nose and cavalryman's thick moustache and looked like an anxious bird with a mouse in its beak. He gave his name as John Brown, used to depart early each day with a salesman's sample-case and return sober at evening.

This for ten weeks was all his landlady knew about him, until one evening he brought a girl home—a demurely spoken young woman, neat as a spike of white hyacinth.

"This lady," he introduced, "is my sister Mary. I am taking her out tonight. Can she wait in my room while I change my collar?" He patted her slim shoulder with a lingering affection unusual in brothers. She was a widow, he explained, her husband having been killed in the war.

They went into Mr. Brown's room, but after a few moments Mary came out. The landlady's daughter found her distressedly clutching the stair-rail.

"I shall be all right, thank you," she said in a thin, ladylike voice. "He—he's shaving—and I can't endure to see that razor —it terrifies me!"

The kindly landlady made her a cup of tea in the kitchen, learned that pretty, vapid Mary Clarke suffered a pathological dread of cut-throat razors, shuddered to glimpse them in shop windows. Of the man who claimed her as his sister, she seemed to know surprisingly little.

Her tea finished, Mary Clarke returned to the lodger's room, found him dressed for the warm July evening in high white collar, cavalry regimental tie, yellow straw hat and sporty gray suit.

"Do not please to wait up for me," he told Mrs. Pannell in his careful foreignish speech. "I am this time remembering to take my key and will wish to open the front door for myself upon returning."

Neither Mrs. Pannell nor her daughter saw the lodger that night nor next day, nor the next. Nearly a week passed. Then, his rent being overdue, Mrs. Pannell tried the door. It was locked.

She hesitated, called the upstairs lodger. "Mr. Grant—can you get into this room for me, please?" adding tartly: "I think our Mr. Brown has done a moonlight!"

Mr. Henry Grant, a sturdy Lancashire chap, examined the door. "I can easy shove it open for you," he said interestedly.

"Pray do no such thing!" declared the landlady. "But you might try his window!"

Henry Grant obediently placed a kitchen chair beneath the lodger's window. The curtains were shut. He began with novice enthusiasm to jab a bread-knife at the window-latch. "Eh, look at all these flies—bluebottles!" he said. "Swarming all over t'window!"

He fumbled the catch open, slid the window up. The hot July afternoon air stirred the drawn curtains. Henry Grant's nose wrinkled. "By gum!" he sniffed critically. He raised the curtain . . . then lowered it dully. His eyes had become shocked. "There's a naked leg stuck out from under t'bed, Mrs. Pannell! And the bed—it's black with blood and flies!"

When Detective-Sergeant Ashbury and his lanky colleague Constable Burscough had lifted the stained bed from the wall, they disclosed the week-dead body of Mary Clarke, clad in torn silk chemise. Her white tender throat was gashed open to the spine. Her torso was startlingly mutilated.

Constable Burscough searched the disordered bedclothes. Blood, like thick tar, darkened them. A disturbed seethe of glutted bluebottles circled and dirged funerally. "There's a bloodstained razor here, Sergeant," he said, his face ashen.

After Mary Clarke's body had been photographed and removed to the mortuary, C.I.D. officers searched the room with expert care.

The lodger, John Brown, had left few traces of himself. In the fireplace, a bit of crumpled envelope bore a penciled scrawl: "s.s. BAKARA." Beneath the paper that lined a lower cupboard shelf was a business card of a licensed broker in Manchester. Behind the tall wardrobe a frayed, and soiled collar, size fifteen and a half, had been discarded. That was all.

Such was the murder report laid upon the desk of Detective-Inspector Arthur L. Jones next day.

"We've identified the woman, sir," said Detective-Sergeant Whitley. "Mary Clarke is her right name, but she's not

Brown's sister. Seems to have been quite a decent girl. None of her friends knew Brown."

Inspector Jones thumbed through the dossier. "Have we checked on this ship the *Bakara?*"

"Yes, sir. I radioed the vessel. The ship was 3,000 miles away when Mary Clarke was murdered. They know nobody like Brown. And this business card, sir—the broker has identified the description of Brown as a salesman, whom he knew as Maurice Ottoman, selling handkerchiefs and table cloths, probably stolen. He says Ottoman called about a month ago, said he was off to take up an offer of a job in a barber shop."

"A barber, eh?" Inspector Jones had been studying the post-mortem medical report, describing the dead girl's drastic mutilations as done "by somebody skilled in use of a razor, and apparently left-handed."

Then, for two days, the C.I.D. searched their city for left-handed barbers with cavalry moustaches. The Police Gazette tally-ho'd the hunt throughout Britain. Nothing was found.

Meanwhile Inspector Arthur Jones, blinking his sailor-blue eyes thoughtfully, was turning in his fingers the soiled collar that had been found behind the wardrobe. It was faintly laundry-marked: "14 BR   40GU   EB."

The landlady, Mrs. Pannell, had already identified the mark "14 BR" as her own address, No. 14 Brownlow Street, and the stamp of the Gem Laundry at Low Hill. The laundry's manager identified "40 GU" as No. 40 Guelph Street.

But there the trail stopped abruptly. For at No. 40 Guelph Street, a respectable neighborhood, the householder—a law-abiding elderly lady named Mrs. Newcombe, emphatically denied ever setting eyes upon a man answering Brown's description. The experienced C.I.D. man who interviewed her came back to police headquarters convinced. "She's a highly respectable lady, sir—what reason could she have to deny it, if she had Brown as a lodger?"

"You never know with ladies," said Inspector Jones, with

the wisdom of a contentedly married man. "I think I'll go and talk to her myself."

His polite tap on the respectably polished door-knocker of No. 40 Guelph Street was answered by Mrs. Newcombe, "I can only repeat that I know nothing," she declared firmly, and at once.

Inspector Jones was unperturbed. "Mind if I come in for a few moments?" he murmured. Mrs. Newcombe shrugged in slight impatience, and perhaps with just a little nervousness, too. Inspector Jones politely doffed his hard bowler hat and entered No. 40 Guelph Street.

Mrs. Newcombe seated herself stiffly against her anti-macassar, hands tight-clasped, lips astringed. Inspector Jones cleared his throat valiantly. . . .

Then a small boy drooped dejected into the room, sobbing. Mrs. Newcombe's grandson, aged eight, had lost his penny down a grid.

Inspector Jones rummaged in his pocket. "Here's sixpence, sonny," he said. The interruption was cheap at the price. Suddenly he saw that Mrs. Newcombe's face had softened. She took the child on to her knee, began to sniff moistly. "Oh, dear," she said, "I've been so worried, Inspector. You look a kindly gentleman . . . I have a confession to make." She went to a cupboard, took down a paper.

"I was afraid to tell the other policemen," she said, "but I *did* have a man here for one week, and he *did* have a moustache like you say, but I never sent his Registration Form to the authorities, Inspector, and when the police came, I was afraid, you see."

"You mean Form A.R.E. under the Defense of the Realm Act?" asked Inspector Jones. "Was this lodger a foreigner?" She nodded guiltily.

Silently, he took the yellow paper from Mrs. Newcombe, and read:

Surname . . . BRAEM. Christian name . . . EDOUARD. Nation-

ality . . . Belgian. Birthplace . . . Courtrai. Date of birth . . .
10-3-73. Present address . . . 40 Guelph Street. Last address . . .
5 Veke Street, Antwerp. Occupation . . . cap-cutter. Served in
Belgian Army (The Lancers).

"You're all right, Ma'am," he said soothingly. "You didn't
have to send this form anywhere, only produce it on demand,
and now you've done that, it's all right."

Then Inspector Jones began a new manhunt—find the
Belgian called Edouard Braem! Alias John Brown! Wanted
for murder!

Central Registry at Home Office had no record of an alien
named Braem. The Aliens' Registry at St. Stephen's House,
Embankment, also reported: "Regret no trace."

So Inspector Jones came personally to New Scotland Yard,
where at that time I was a raw young constable of not quite a
fortnight's service, and my helmet strap still rubbed my chin
sore.

Inspector Jones was a water-polo International, huge-
chested, could stay under water three minutes, and his eyes
were metallic as blue steel rivets.

"I'm seeking an alien," he said, "named Edouard Braem."

We had the name on the Yard's C.R.O. File: Braem—three
months in 1915 for failing to register as an alien. Inspector
Jones took a photograph back to Liverpool with him, and
Mrs. Pannell, Mrs. Newcombe, Mr. Henry Grant and others,
identified it positively as the murderous John Brown.

But where was he? Inspector Jones obtained authority to
search records of the Central Registry of Shipping and inquired at every British seaport . . . the man Edouard Braem
had crossed to Ostend via Dover on July 21—the day after the
dead girl was discovered!

Detective-Chief-Superintendent McCoy of Liverpool Police
sailed at once for Antwerp, reported to the Chief Police Commissioner in that city, and was taken by Inspector de Rooke
at six a.m. to No. 5 Veke Street—a squalid café. Braem was in

bed, in yet another back room. The officers found a bloodstained shirt, and two cuttings from English newspapers of
the murder. They arrested him.

"But I didn't kill her," protested Braem. "It was done by a
man named Fischer who lives in Manchester."

This was clever. It raised a doubt. Braem described Fischer
as small, staring blue eyes, Australian-born, aged thirty-six.
Fischer had cut her throat and dumped her under the bed
while he, Braem, was drunk. Next morning, Fischer having
disappeared, Braem became terrified and fled.

This statement was cabled back to Liverpool. Inspector
Jones drew a heavy sigh into his tremendous lungs, and went
doggedly in search of a small, blue-eyed Australian named
Fischer. There was only one way to do it. He had to seek out
ever Fischer or Fisher in Liverpool and Manchester, and if he
failed in those two cities . . . try the rest of England.

Amazingly, after four weeks, he actually discovered one
Harry Fisher who was prepared to admit that he knew Braem.
Also, he answered every detail of the description. There was
just one flaw—he could prove he hadn't killed Mary Clarke.

That seemed to leave Braem again as No. 1 Suspect. Inspector Jones visited Sir Early Blackwell, Permanent Under
Secretary of State at the Home Office, to request Braem's
extradition from Belgium to stand trial at Liverpool for murder.

"Can't be done, Inspector," said Sir Early. "Have a cigar.
This chap's a Belgian, and there is no death penalty in Bel-
gium. So he can successfully appeal against being shipped to
England to risk the death sentence here."

What now? Liverpool Police dealt with this new setback
with typical northern doggedness. They put their seventeen
witnesses on board ship, in charge of Inspector Jones, who
bore the appropriate exhibits in a leather hatbox, and sailed
the lot to Antwerp! "If we can't try him for murder here," they
said, "We'll try him on his own soil!"

They did. On July 11, 1922—one year after Braem had
murdered Mary Clarke in Liverpool, a jury of his own country-

men in Antwerp found him guilty, after a procession of Liverpool witnesses had given their testimony. Braem was sentenced
to penal servitude for life, loss of political rights, forfeit £1,096
expenses for his trial . . . and the seventeen witnesses sailed
home to Liverpool, still under the guardian eye of Inspector
Arthur Jones of that city's police force.

JOHNNY CALDWELL REMOVED HIS SHOES and climbed the drainpipe to an open bathroom window. A loaded Colt pistol sagged his pocket. The house was dark. The householders—at that time of night—were probably at the cinema. It was eight p.m. on a windy March night, 1946.

If they returned to surprise him, the gun would hold them off. It had done in previous burglaries.

Mr. and Mrs. James Deckan, returning at eight-ten p.m. from first-house pictures, were surprised to see a light in their bedroom. Mr. Deckan's latch-key would not open the lock. He hurried next door. "Fetch your truncheon, Jim," he said anxiously. "I've got burglars!"

His neighbor, elderly Mr. James Straiton, had been a detective-sergeant in the Glasgow Police Force. He was not, therefore, afraid of burglars. For years he had kept his old police baton, in hope. . . .

Upstairs in the bedroom, pockets bulged with loot, Johnny

Caldwell heard something, came softly on stocking-feet to the stairs. Two solemn Glasgow householders, both gray-haired, were waiting for him. "All right, sonny," said the taller man, "better put down that gun."

Johnny Caldwell twisted his girlishly pretty young mouth into a sneer. Deliberately he raised the pistol to Mr. Deckan's stomach. "You let me through—or he'll get it!"

Mr. Deckan, with stubborn courage, stood firm. Johnny Caldwell fired. The bullet whisked Deckan's sleeve, thudded into the wall. Deckan winced back, and, lithe as an alley-cat, Caldwell dashed into the gap that led to freedom. . . .

He had barely taken one step when the inside of his skull seemed to explode. Johnny Caldwell stumbled to his knees among a mist of red and silver stars. Ex-Detective-Sergeant Straiton had clouted him scientifically behind the ear with his little detective's baton.

Once upon a time that would have closed the incident. Glasgow policemen using truncheons large or small, are seldom to be mistaken for poets waving daffodils. In skill, valor, Straiton had not diminished. But the years had sapped his arm. Johnny Caldwell rose from his knees, fired twice—darted for the street.

Behind him, elderly Mr. James Straiton writhed and died upon his neighbor's stair-carpet. It was murder.

In the gutter down Edinburgh Road, investigating C.I.D. officers found watches, trinkets, belonging to Mr. Deckan. The unknown thief had cast away his loot as he dodged into oblivion. Nor were there fingerprints.

"He was a chap about twenty-five years old," said Deckan, shakily. "A pale face. Smallish to medium size. He wore a light grey tweed overcoat, a white scarf and cap."

Police dug the bullet from the stair wall. There were two more in Straiton. A pair of shoes were found alongside the bathroom drainpipe. Three bullets, a pair of crumpled black size-eight shoes, and a vague description. This was all the Glasgow Police had.

"The bullets were from a Colt .45," said Chief Inspector George McLean of the Police Science Department. "The shoes are about three years old, belonged to a person very young, extremely active."

For five fruitless days, Glasgow Police sought the murderer. Their underworld gave no clues. Nor had any respectable citizen glimpsed a young man without shoes, hastening away from the district of Edinburgh Road.

"Delay much more and we've lost him," said Chief Superintendent William Ewing, who had picked up his city by the scruff and shaken it skilfully for nearly a week, without one further clue dropping forth.

His assistant, Detective-Superintendent Gilbert J. McIlvrick, spoke bluntly as he always did: "We should abandon the murder-hunt, and start looking for the burglar!"

"That's it!" said Ewing. "The murder was the work of an instant, without thought—but the burglary was premeditated, and expert. Let's have a look at the Method Index."

They turned up: "HOUSEBREAKING—methods of gaining entry —drainpipe climbing." (In Glasgow they are called "rone-pipes.") Somebody had climbed a drain-pipe to rob a house in Whitehall Street, eight days before the murder. The thief had splintered open a heavy cupboard with some unusually forcible tool.

Detective-Superintendent McIlvrick went to examine this house. The thief had climbed to a bedroom window, opened it with a penknife. Stuck in the wood beneath the window-catch, McIlvrick found the tiny end of a knife-blade. In the splintered lock of the cupboard, he discovered a squashed bullet. The lock had been exploded by a pistol shot! The battered bullet was taken for examination.

"That bullet was fired by the murder gun," said Detective-Inspector James McLellan, M.A., B.Sc., A.R.I.C., finally switching off the microscope light in the police laboratory.

Nobody had seen the burglar who robbed the house in Whitehall Street. But, further back in the Method Index, not under "DRAINPIPE," but filed among: "GUNS—housebreakers using," was a robbery at Golfhill Drive. This was a ground-floor flat.

A window had been broken. The lady occupant had re turned, surprised the thief, who threatened her successfully with a gun, and escaped. She described him: "Age about twenty to twenty-four years, slim and pale, wearing a light-grey tweed overcoat, white scarf and cap."

Gun . . . grey tweed overcoat . . . white scarf . . . cap. All matched with the murderer.

"Anything else?" asked McIlvrick.

"Yes, sir—a bit of a fingerprint, found on a piece of broken glass from the window," said Detective-Sergeant Douglas Hamilton, quietly. "But it was not big enough for identification."

By police custom, a fingerprint found at a crime-scene must compare to sixteen points with a fingerprint on file, making a 4,200 million to 1 chance against error, before it is "identifiable." The fingerprint smudge found on the broken glass was not much bigger than a gnat's wing.

"Yes, I think, from its position, that this is a thumb-print," said Chief Inspector MacLean.

From the 98,000 cards of recorded thumbprints in Glasgow C.I.D., were sorted all those of men convicted for housebreaking. There were thousands of them.

"Reduce those," said MacLean, "to all the housebreakers between twenty and thirty years old."

"Make it eighteen years old," put in McIlvrick, who had remembered MacLean's own words about the shoes found on the murder scene—"probably worn by a person *very* young." That left 450 cards.

"Now," said MacLean, "I think we can take out the cards of the men still in prison, or with similarly good alibis."

His assistants restored sixty cards to the closely-crammed green filing cabinets.

"What about chaps in Borstal?" inquired a zealous detective-constable, anxious not to do the wrong thing.

"No!" said Chief Superintendent Ewing, surprisingly.

"Leave all the Borstal lads, for sorting. I know something about Borstal—they get holidays—compassionate leave, early discharges for good conduct—heaven knows what else!"

The stiff white card that contained the fingerprints of nineteen-year-old Johnny Caldwell, in theory still serving a Borstal term of three years, was put back in the heap to be examined.

"Now, let's get going," said MacLean.

They worked all that day, and all night. All next day (it was Sunday) and the next night. The scrap of fingerprint on the smashed window-glass was far too small for a proper index search. It had to be matched like a jigsaw piece.

Lanky, quiet-spoken Detective-Sergeant Douglas Hamilton, on the afternoon of the third sleepless day, suddenly pushed back his chair with, for him, a startling oath.

"I'll eat my damned hat if—" He held up a card.

The others gathered around him. The tiny smudge of fingerprint, no larger than a toenail paring, found on the burglary scene, did seem to match one corner of the left-hand thumbprint of—CALDWELL, J.—serving a Borstal term!

A C.I.D. car whisked to Caldwell's house. Johnny was there, taken completely by surprise. In his pocket, a pen-knife with a broken tip. Under police microscopes, it matched exactly the bit of blade found at the burglary scene where the pistol shot had been fired into the cupboard . . . and this bullet matched the murder gun. The chain of evidence was there.

At Barlinnie Prison, Glasgow, on August 10, 1946, John Caldwell, then just twenty years old, was hanged.

THE TINY CHINESE LADY WHOSE NAME was Wai-Sheung Siu, was undoubtedly a clever girl, though not much taller than a daffodil. Yet even a clever girl can make the mistake of marrying a murderer.

Her father was a rich mandarin near Hong Kong. He had twenty children. His Number One Wife died when little Wai-Sheung Siu was eleven years old, and the schoolgirl daughter was put in complete charge of the big household and its funds.

Her father's concubines bent resigned, slender necks behind their ivory fans. Even her proud brothers did no more than stir silk sleeves in a shrug of acquiescence. For Wai-Sheung Siu was such a clever girl!

She found time to go to America and graduate from Boston University. When her father himself died, young Wai-Sheung Siu hurried home from London where she had been showing Chinese works of art, and opened shops that sold antiques to

Americans. Before her twenty-fifth birthday she was practically the richest woman in China. She was blithe, polite, her slant bronze eyes unwaveringly bright. A big man might almost have put the tiny, pretty creature in his poacher's pocket. She remained unwed. Most of the young men were afraid of her wealth, her mandarin ancestry. Some, of her cleverness.

But when at a party in New York she met young Chung Yi Miao, a newly qualified doctor of laws, aged twenty-eight, he did not drop his almond eyes before any of these dazzling virtues. Indeed, they widened. For he was smart, too. His father had been a mandarin, too.

As for money—Mr. Chung Yi Miao had only £400. He put this into a New York bank, drew out £390, put this in another bank, drew out £350, put it in another bank, drew out . . .

When careful friends of the rich little Wai-Sheung Siu asked him, in that deadly calm, patient way of Chinese gentlemen who wish to know, about his finances, Mr. Chung Yi Miao was able to flourish a fistful of paying-in slips and check-books, and indeed seemed to have accounts with most of the banks in New York!

So that was all right. In her private diary, Miss Wai-Sheung Siu wrote: "October 10: . . . He is very good-looking and has very pleasant manners and seems quite different from all other boys. I became quite interested . . ."

"October 11: . . . I am very much in love now . . ."

"October 12: . . . I think he loves me . . ."

Within seven months her private, blossom-scented diary had fluttered its rice-pages to show:

"May 12. This is my wedding day. The wedding was beautiful but I felt so lonely for him all morning. . . . I wept on my way to the hairdresser's place in Fifth Avenue. . . ."

"May 14. . . . Stayed at the Penn Hotel for two nights now. I love my husband very much . . ."

The wedding had been a star event in New York society. The Chinese Consul-General was best man. The tall, handsome groom; his young bride so tiny that the lilies-of-the-valley in her bouquet seemed big as white tulips in her little hand.

The blaze of her jewelry at the reception party caused New York cops to twitch guns in belt-holsters and glare thoughtfully at the crowd.

They went for a honeymoon on a world tour that was to end in China. America—Canada—Scotland—the English Lake District, where they arrived on a showery June day, to take rooms at the Borrowdale Grange Hotel.

There had not been a murder in Cumberland for nearly forty years, and neither the happy little heiress nor the hospitable folk of Keswick were even thinking of murder that day, as the summer rain made petit-point on Derwentwater, and the distant hills shone blue under a clearer sky.

But two men had murder on their minds. One was Detective-Constable William Pendelbury, on holiday from the Southport Borough Police. The other was a handsome Chinese doctor of laws.

"What a lovely place for a murder," said C.I.D. Officer Pendlebury, as he surveyed the beautiful quietness of Cummacatta Wood.

His young wife dug a playful elbow in his ribs. "Go on," she said. "You give me the creeps—and besides, you're on holiday!"

That same afternoon, Dr. Chung Yi Miao also surveyed the same stretch of almost trackless woods, from Grange Bridge, and there was a serene smile on his Oriental face. Who can tell what a Chinaman is thinking? His tiny bride clung warmly to his arm.

An hour and a half later, Detective-Constable Pendlebury, whose eyes just would not take a holiday, saw a tall young Chinaman walking quickly up the road by Grange Bridge. A camera was slung across his shoulder, and he was alone. This was the first time Pendlebury had ever seen Dr. Chung Yi Miao.

At his hotel, Dr. Miao told the proprietress, Miss Crossley:

"My wife has gone to Keswick to buy warmer underclothes. She will be back for tea."

She was not. Everybody at the hotel was impressed at the way Dr. Miao worried for his little wife, when it became six o'clock. By nine o'clock, he was distraught, and wanted to phone the police.

He need not have bothered, for by nine o'clock that excellent police officer, Pendlebury, had already found his wife. She lay on her back among the woods. A string was knotted tightly around her little throat, knotted under the ear. She was dead, legs sprawled, clothing disarranged, a brown umbrella covering her face and upper body. Her left hand showed scratches where two rings had been brutally torn away.

She might have been attacked. She seemed to have been robbed. She had certainly been strangled.

The tireless Pendlebury had gone back to the lonely night woods from the cozy warmth of Grange village tavern for no other reason than a farmer saying: "I saw a woman lying near Kidham Dub, under an umbrella, this evening. Funny thing, eh—in the rain, an' all!" Often to his wife's despair, a good policeman just doesn't know how to take a holiday!

When Inspector Graham of Cumberland Police, having thus been given a flying start by his colleague from Southport, came to the Borrowdale Grange Hotel, at eleven p.m., he found Dr. Miao in bed. "Your wife," he said, after the formal preliminaries, "has been found strangled in a wood near Grange Bridge."

Dr. Miao became emotional. "What? My wife—robbed and murdered?"

Nobody had said anything about her being robbed. Thankful that he had administered the official caution before receiving this valuable evidence, Inspector Graham promptly arrested Dr. Miao, sent him under escort to Keswick Police Station, and began to search the bedroom. He found £4,000-worth of the murdered bride's jewelry. The jewel-case keys were in Dr.

Miao's bag, but the two diamond rings, which all the other guests and servants of the hotel had noticed, were not there.

This was the bulwark of Dr. Miao's indignant defense. "She was always displaying her jewels. Somebody saw her diamonds. She was robbed and killed. What motive had I to rob her? In Chinese law I own all her property."

As for his going to bed, Dr. Miao explained he had a severe cold. And he had.

"I did not tell to the Police Inspector," he lisped truculently, "that my wife had been 'robbed and murdered.' I said 'rudely murdered.'"

Yet, despite all this, the Keswick police were sure Dr. Miao had done the murder. They started to pull his defense to fragments, slowly, carefully, and—even though they had not seen a murder in forty years—expertly.

"Firstly," said police surgeon Dr. Crawford, "the pressure on the string shows that the murderer had been standing just behind her, at her right side. No signs of a struggle. So, unless he completely surprised her, she must have known and trusted him.

"She was killed instantly. Her body then rolled, several feet, down from the flat rock. The bruises show she had been sat on the rock. The string is not jerked upward, and she is a tiny woman. So the murderer must have been sitting almost alongside her."

Then came an expert in Forensic Medicine—Professor John McFall of Liverpool.

"Although the dead woman's gloves were found neatly beside the body, as if she might have been carrying them, and therefore displaying her diamond rings, nevertheless they were not removed from the hands by the woman herself," he said. "Look at the finger-ends! They are not pinched!

"Now, a woman, Chinese or English, first loosens her tight gloves at the finger-ends. These, however, were pulled off from the wrists."

So . . . the gloves had been removed by the murderer to get

at the rings. The murderer could not have been a casual thief, who had glimpsed the valuable sparkle, and snatched for it. Where, indeed, were those rings? The police began a careful search.

"Get the film in that camera developed," said Inspector Graham. "You never know—it might contain a clue."

A local photographer was given the job. He unwound the half-finished spool that had been in the camera of Dr. Miao which Detective Pendlebury had spotted—and found six photographs of Scottish scenery! That was a disappointment. But in the camera case was a spare roll of film. "I don't think this has been used," said the photographer.

"There's one good way of finding out," said Inspector Graham tersely. "Open it up!"

The photographer unwrapped the silver-paper—and there, concealed on the spool beneath the wrapping, were two rings! They fitted the tiny dead hand of Wai-Sheung Siu.

There was only one thing now to discover—what on earth had been the motive? Her scented, dainty diary, with its little love-story, perishable as a snowflake, gave the answer. Soon after her marriage, Wai-Sheung Siu had written forlornly: "Today the doctor gives me bad news."

The doctor in America, was traced. "Sure," he said, "I attended her." His voice crackled across the trans-Atlantic phone. "I told her she could never have a baby."

And there it was. Dr. Miao had wed his heiress. His technique had been Western almost to the point of roguery. That business with the New York banks, for instance. But when it came to being denied rightful sons, the honorable ancestors of Dr. Miao rose accusingly. He was the son of a mandarin, and must perpetuate his ancient lineage.

Dr. Miao waited, took his barren bride through America, Canada, Scotland—to the English Lakes. The austere English, he thought, would never understand such a motive. . . .

But they understood only too well. He was hanged at Strangeways.

The Case of the Skilful Doctor

THE JEALOUS BROWN THUMBS OF DR.
Buck Ruxton had crushed into his wife's white neck in previous quarrels. Usually, as she gasped and writhed, he wept
for shame at his own passion, begged her with kisses to pardon
him.

This night (September 14, 1935) his wrath endured a
heartbeat too long, his clever thumbs dug too fiercely into her
throat. She died between his hands. Not merely a dark bruise
to kiss away . . . a dead wife, this time, sprawled head down
upon the stairway at No. 2 Dalton Square, Lancaster: horror
frozen into her eyes like red moths in amber.

Such was Dr. Buck Ruxton's problem now. He leaned and
panted against his red-and-white ornamental stairway. In two
seconds he had become a murderer. No kiss would wipe out
that!

He heard bare feet scuffle on the upper landing. Mary the
young housemaid had been watching and had seen Isobel

Ruxton die: Dr. Buck Ruxton walked carefully up the bend of
the stairs towards the young girl, all the time speaking to her
softly as one might coax an apprehensive dog into a sack for
drowning. In her bedroom he seized and struck her. She fell,
staring wildly up at the room's ceiling pattern of bursting
silver stars.

Now Dr. Ruxton had two dead women in his house. It was
midnight. The tall gray police station of Lancaster town was
across the square, the towers of its jail were on the dark
horizon. He could see the police-station lights as he lifted the
curtain of his front bedroom window. He should now walk
across that square, leave behind the orientally decorated house
that was his pride, and surrender to the police.

An English gentleman would surely do no less. Dr. Buck
Ruxton, whose black skin troubled him like a hole in the sock,
like a bleeding nose on a public platform, cared very much
about the correct behavior of a gentleman.

He was a Parsee Indian from Bombay, with a touch of
French blood in him, and a vast hunger to be what he was not.
He had invented for his wife (she was a waitress) a titled
grandfather, boasted that his own dark veins held blue blood
of Scottish kings.

He lowered the curtain, shut out the view of the police
station. Be his blood blue or red, it was not cool enough to
walk across that empty square and surrender to the hangman.

All Dr. Ruxton's blood was hot. Very hot. Tantrums, kind-
ness, smiles, tempers, tears . . . a dappled pattern. Saturday
picnics for the town's orphaned kiddies in his bright new car,
white with blue wheels. "The sky's the limit! Let us enjoy a
run!" The same night in a sick-room kneeling in fastidious
pin-stripe trousers at a patient's bedside, praying aloud with
tear-wet cheeks: "Oh God, restore the boon of health to this
lady, work Thy miracles through my humble medical skill."
But in those two minutes on the stairs both charity and God
had been forgotten. It was murder.

Dr. Buck Ruxton drew a ragged breath, lit a cigarette,
decided to fight for his life. He was a clever doctor.

At Bombay University he had taken, among other distinctions, one in forensic medicine—the art by which doctors understand how to tell murder from suicide, bruises of attack from wounds self-inflicted, how to identify corpses. He would use his medical skill to fight the vast clumsy machine of British law . . . and the police across the square, who used to say: "G'morning, Doctor" with a gleam of amused pity in their eyes because they knew about his debts, his bad temper, his extravagances of clean shirt, socks, underwear each day, and how his wife had twice run away from him and the three children, after quarrels. . . .

Yes, she had twice run away—and suddenly Dr. Ruxton saw clearly his way of escape. She must be made to seem to have run away again! This time take the maid with her. They would never come back, never be seen again. Why, he would even ask the police to search for them, oh yes, he would be clever.

The first thing was get rid of both bodies. Dr. Buck Ruxton knew the law: "In the absence of actual evidence of the accused killing the person, he has no onus to account for the disappearance of the person alleged to have been killed." Hide the bodies and you hide the crime!

He knew too much to bury them in the house, or under the firm flagstones of the yard. Police always found such guilty graves.

He dragged the dead girl downstairs into the bathroom, then carried the stark body of the woman he had loved, up the stairs and laid her on the black-and-white checkered bathroom linoleum. Their three children slept on, in three cots around her empty bed.

He put Mary Rogerson into the bath. One blue eye had a recognizable squint. He removed both. He chopped away her hair. Police descriptions would call it "light brown." Ruxton swilled hanks of light brown hair down the domestic drains.

Then he remembered his textbooks. A quarter-inch of human hair is rooted below the skin surface. He slid his wafer-thin blue blade around the scalp. A birthmark of red patches

on her right arm. He cut it away. Deftly with glistening
scalpel he removed lips, ears, nose. Her face had freckles.
Buxton skinned the face. Relatives would not recognize red
flesh.

Now a skilled operation. The quick knife cut deep. The
dead needed no anesthetic. Man or woman . . . who could
now tell? Downstairs, for teeth-forceps out of his sterilized
white cabinet. Cut up the body at each articulate joint. Slick
dismemberment. No vulgar hacksaws for this pupil of the
Royal College of Surgeons at Edinburgh.

Then, his wife, Isobel Ruxton had long nails. He cut off
each first finger-joint. Her legs were notoriously thick. He
sliced flesh from knee to foot. She had been treated for in-
flamed bunions on left big toe. Ruxton removed the toes.

This woman he had loved. He began to be sick with more
than fear. The bathroom's black-and-white *décor* whirled into
a vortex. . . . When he opened his eyes, his blue suit was
mottled with blood. His gold wrist-watch told him the time
was six-thirty a.m. Gray dawn had crept into Dalton Square.
In half an hour the charwoman would arrive:

He scrambled into a brown overcoat, drove to the house of
Mrs. Agnes Oxley. Her sleepy husband answered the bell.
Mrs. Oxley blinked, hair becurlered, on the stairs.

"Tell Mrs. Oxley not to come this morning," smiled Dr.
Ruxton. "My wife and her maid have gone to Edinburgh and
I am taking the children to Morecambe this afternoon."

He returned to the house. His children were still asleep.
Now he saw blood, on stairs and carpets. He hadn't remembered this blood . . . but there it was!

Dr. Buck Ruxton slid his scalpel bravely across the fingers
of his own right hand. "I cut it on a tin-opener," he said, re-
hearsing himself.

That would account for the blood!

He took the children to stay with friends. "My wife has left
me," he explained piteously.

The blue suit, and bloodstained carpets he gave to one of
his poor patients. Shrewder than attempting to destroy them.

"Cut out the tailor's name from the suit," he said. "Burn it. It's undignified for a man to wear a suit with another man's name in it." Clever Dr. Ruxton, with a glib answer for everything!

He told Mary Rogerson's parents: "The poor girl was going to have a baby. My wife took her away with her. They took £30 from my safe." That shameful news would stun the Rogersons to silence for a while.

And now, the disposal. He had cut the two bodies into nearly a hundred parts. These he wrapped in parcels. He used a sheet from his wife's bed (careful to see there were no laundry marks). He used old newspapers. Some old rags, a pillow slip, wads of cotton wool.

There was a deep ravine at Moffat, on a bleak and desolate part of the Edinburgh-Carlisle Road. He had motored over it and remembered it now, in his hour of need, four years later. Clever Dr. Ruxton! A torrent seethed through the ravine below Gardenholme Bridge, among a ten-foot high tangle of pathless vegetation. He grasped the parapet and peered into the ravine below, at its rain-swollen stream. It seemed safe to drop a thousand bloodstained parcels over such a bridge and hope never to see them again.

In his hired and anonymous Austin Dr. Ruxton then drove 300 miles home through night and daybreak to Lancaster, satisfied. . . .

Home, in Dalton Square, in the back yard that no eye in Lancaster could overlook, he burned a few bloodstained oddments, then washed his hands carefully. The job was done. It was the perfect murder—by clever Dr. Ruxton!

That dawn the rain deluge dramatically ceased. For the next two September weeks, surprising drought shriveled Gardenholme stream . . . until the river banks became crusted mud. Upon this mud a torn parcel lay visibly stuck.

A girl, daydreaming on the bridge, saw it. "Surely—that's a human hand!"

Ponderous Scots policemen that afternoon trampled the gulley bracken, splashed the thin river, and 600 yards downstream discovered other bundles. Maggots squirmed in them.

"Maggots—excellent!" beamed Professor John Glaister of Glasgow University, as he viewed the pulpy parcels. "Such muscid larvae will indicate almost the precise hour of death and of abandonment!"

The assorted human fragments were sent to Dr. Gilbert Millar's laboratory at Edinburgh, for identification.

"Not thrown in the ravine by a local man," commented Inspector Strath of the Dumfries Police. "The river runs to one side of the bridge parapet except in flood. That's why the parcel was left stranded when the rain stopped."

Professor Glaister blinked at the seventy fragments, spectacles halfway down his shrewd nose. "Cleverly dissected," he said. "Certainly by someone with medical skill!"

His colleague Professor James Brash spent fascinated weeks jig-sawing the bits together. "Two bodies," he decided. "One complete torso still missing, and two feet, also a hand and forearm."

Bloodhounds failed to trace the missing pieces, but a shepherd found one of the feet among bracken ten miles away. Its toes were amputated.

"Why remove toes from one foot only?" Glaister and Brash asked each other. "Was there some abnormality the murderer was trying to conceal?"

From one head, lips and tongue-tip had been shorn. "Therefore this woman was probably strangled," guessed Glaister. "These are the parts that would have shown strangulation signs."

"Observe the soot deposits in the lungs," said Brash. "Evidently town dwellers." Also, congestion's specks, confirming death cause as strangulation in at least one victim.

"Both bodies had been carefully mutilated. "So how can you be sure if they are men or women, particularly with one complete torso missing?" asked a police official.

"The larynx—the voice-box," said Glaister. "No adam's-apple—also the tilt of the thigh-joints."

"One of these skulls is that of a woman about twenty years old," said Brash. "The other is about thirty-five. Note the difference in skull-sutures—that soft spot on top of each head that is wide open in newborn babies and shuts gradually as we get older."

Meanwhile the police had examined the wrappings of the hideous parcels. Some old newspapers, straw, rags, cotton wool, a patched white blouse of cheap georgette without laundry marks. One torn bit of newspaper was a page of the *Sunday Graphic,* dated September 15. A partly obliterated headline: "AMBE'S CARNIVAL QUEEN CROWNED," and two photos.

Superintendent Adam M'Laren was aware that national big-circulation newspapers print differing editions for various parts of the country. A Scottish edition of the *Sunday Graphic* would hardly be likely to carry two photos of Morecambe's carnival queen.

Mr. Edwin Vaughan Morris, circulation manager of the *Sunday Graphic,* confirmed: "That is a copy of our special 'slip' edition for Morecambe and Lancaster. Only 3,700 copies printed."

"Any missing women in your areas?" the police chiefs of Morecambe and Lancaster were promptly asked.

"Yes," answered Chief Constable H. J. Vann of Lancaster. "Mrs. Ruxton, aged thirty-five, wife of a doctor, and her maid Mary, aged twenty."

"Any peculiarities of toes in either woman?"

Mr. Vann replied: "Yes, Mrs. Ruxton had deformed toes."

"When were the women reported missing?"

"September 16."

The copy of the *Sunday Graphic* was September 15! All further investigation was at once placed in charge of Chief Constable Vann of Lancaster.

"How many copies of that special 'slip' edition came to Lancaster?" he immediately asked, and was told 728 copies, one being delivered to the house of Dr. Buck Ruxton.

The patched white georgette blouse, in which two bits of

arm had been swathed, was cleaned and displayed to Mary Rogerson's mother, who recognized it.

"I bought it at a jumble sale for Mary. Look"—she lifted the sleeve—"that's the patch I sewed on!"

Meanwhile, Dr. Buck Ruxton, anxious and restless, bobbed in to Lancaster police station. "Look here, Vann, haven't you found my wife yet?" He brandished a newspaper. "It's outrageous—they're trying to say those two bodies in Scotland are my wife and Mary Rogerson. It's ruining my practice! You must stop the newspapers from publishing such lies!"

"What makes you so sure it isn't true, doctor?" asked Vann carefully.

Ruxton's dark eyes glittered. "Well, here it says the younger of the two dead women found in Scotland has a full set of teeth in the lower jaw, and *I know of my own knowledge,* that both my wife and Mary Rogerson had teeth missing!"

Chief Constable Vann was thus armed with another clue. All that afternoon police teleprinters clattered between Lancaster and Scotland, where Dr. A. C. W. Hutchinson, Dean of Edinburgh Dental School, was investigating the teeth of the two dead women.

"Several teeth extracted after death," reported Dr. Hutchinson. "I have reproduced the false teeth that must have been worn by body No. 2 (Mrs. Ruxton): left upper lateral incisor canine and first pre-molar."

To the police that evening, Lancaster dentist John Thistlethwaite, examining the dental plate reproduced by Dr. Hutchinson, said: "This matches exactly the one I made two years ago for Mrs. Ruxton. Left upper lateral incisor, canine and first pre-molar."

Soon, Detective-Inspector Bill Thompson reported to his chief, *re* Ruxton: "I think chummie across the Square is getting a bit desperate. Remember he has a revolver in that house, Sir!"

Chief Constable Vann looked at his calendar. It was October 12. "I think it's time we had him over here," he said, and picked up the phone.

"Dr. Ruxton? It's Vann here. Those newspaper stories you complained about—I think we can put an end to that sort of nuisance for you, doctor. Why not come and see me tonight?"

Dr. Ruxton, delighted and hopeful, rushed bareheaded across Dalton Square, thumped on the heavy mahogany door of Chief Constable Vann's private office. A quiet voice said "Come in."

Dr. Ruxton bounded in. "Ah, Vann, I'm so glad . . . ," his shrill, Oriental voice trailed into silence. At the Chief Constable's big desk sat a row of senior police officials. They gazed at Ruxton in solemn pity. One moved to the door, and shut it. . . .

That night he was charged with murder. And on March 12, 1935, at Manchester Assizes began an eleven-day trial that was to become an all-time classic for its disclosure of painstaking police investigation.

One hundred and eight prosecution witnesses detailed every move that Ruxton had made since his wife disappeared. Police reports, in typed foolscap, stacked fourteen inches high on the Prosecutor's table. The laboratory findings of the team of scientists comprised two written books and 300 photographs.

The skull found at Gardenholme ravine was superimposed upon the photos of Mrs. Ruxton, with scale-size, checked by her jeweled tiara, put across each forehead. The bones of the dead woman, echoing every curve of the known face of Mrs. Ruxton, peered out of the photographs to the jury like an accusing ghost.

Plaster casts of the dead women's feet were fitted exactly into well-worn shoes of Mrs. Ruxton and Mary Rogerson. They matched each bulge and wrinkle. Even palm prints recovered skilfully from one peeled dead hand were matched with hand prints found on a dish in the Ruxton household.

A flaw in the weft of one piece of cotton sheet that had
wrapped the corpse fragments, was shown to match an identical flaw in the sheet on Mrs. Ruxton's own bed. Experts
testified that the sheets must have been made on the same
loom from the same bobbin, and cut consecutively from the
same piece of cloth.

Blood was traced in the bathroom drains. There was enough
evidence to hang the medical murderer twenty times.

On May 12, 1935, at Strangeways Prison, Manchester, that
good doctor and bad husband, Dr. Buck Ruxton, died by
judicial hanging, giving the one life he had for the two he
had taken.

THE LITTLE FOREIGNER SPAT A MOUTHFUL
of blood into the dentist's bowl. His brown, rather childlike
eyes were gratefully bright. He watched the dentist examine
the extracted tooth.

"Bad—ver' bad, nein?" Little Mr. Veltman could hardly
speak English.

"No signs of decay," said the dentist. "But as it caused you
such pain you are better without it." He laid the tooth on
cotton wool. "I'll give you a bottle of mouthwash . . ." he
illustrated with gestures. Mr. Veltman nodded his dark face
eagerly.

"Ja—ja, I pay!" He fumbled in his bulging jacket, pulled out
a pebble of grey cement, broke off a corner.

The dentist, Mr. Paul, was surprised to see a gleaming edge
of gold. Little Veltman rubbed at the cement until he extracted

a complete gold coin, like a nut from chocolate. The dentist could see other gleams of gold in the cement.

"Enough—plenty, plizz?" Veltman proffered the gold coin doubtfully. "More?" He motioned towards the cement block.

The dentist examined the coin. A genuine South African currency piece—a Rand Sovereign. At that time—September 1936—any gold sovereign was worth at least £1 13s. 6d.

"You need some change—I mean, my fee is ten shillings—see, ten—no, dash it, not ten of those coins, put 'em away—I mean, this coin is a sovereign—*twenty* shillings—no, no—oh, for heaven's sake . . ."

Little Mr. Veltman did at last seem to get the idea that the gold sovereign in some way equalled a £1 note, and yet in some strange way was worth more than £1 to the dentist.

"Iss goot!" he beamed. "Tomorrow my friend bring more. You pay £1 for each, hein?"

The dentist, slightly startled at his own good fortune, nodded.

Next day, Veltman brought a tall, taciturn companion in dazzling pearl-gray hat, neatly pressed suit, who peered from behind a huge black moustache. Both were Austrian refugees, had discovered the gold coins while doing forced demolition work for the Nazis. They hid the treasure—2,000 Rand Sovereigns—in a sack of cement, had managed to smuggle them ashore at Plymouth.

Offers by the dentist of more than £1 each for the coins seemed to arouse instant distrust. They reluctantly agreed to £2,300, to be paid after Mr. Paul had examined each coin. It took him four days to raise the cash. Veltman bobbed in daily, suspicious at such delay.

At last Mr. Paul was able to show the money. £2,000 in £50 banknotes, and £300 in singles, all stacked crisp in his safe. Little Veltman departed, came back in half an hour with his tall comrade, who was now tilted sideways by a heavy gladstone bag, bulging with pebbles of cement.

"More to come," he grunted, sweating. "Could not carry. Iss money here?"

Mr. Paul patiently showed him. The tall man produced a large red handkerchief, wrapped the money in it, appeared to put this precious bundle in the gladstone bag, locked it dramatically.

"This," he held up the key, "we keep. That—" he jerked a thumb at the bag, "you keep. Now I fetch more."

For an hour Mr. Paul waited, then wrenched open the bag. The red handkerchief . . . contained only new paper! The cement pebbles were, of course, just cement pebbles. Mr. Paul reported his victimization at once to Plymouth police.

Detective-Superintendent William T. Hutchings flung a circle of radio cars around Plymouth's exits. The two swindlers had ninety minutes' start. Detectives rushed to railway stations, bus terminals, airports, searched the harbor vessels. A police launch churned the night waters of Plymouth Sound. There was no trace of the two men with the £2,300. Hutchings turned to the Police Gazette and Method Index to see if such a trick had been attempted before.

Swindlers always repeat themselves. Three months previously at Leeds, he found, a man known as Hagendorf, who had a criminal record, had robbed a doctor of £385 with brass buttons embedded in cement. His photo had already been circulated by Leeds police. Superintendent Hutchings studied the photo, thoughtfully penciled in a large, Stalinesque moustache.

"That's the big man!" said the dentist eagerly.

Plymouth Police circulated a new photo of Hagendorf, this time with moustache.

The other clue Hutchings had was that little Veltman must have kept his gladstone bag and confederate somewhere within fifteen minutes of Mr. Paul's house, else he could not have produced both within thirty minutes of being told the money awaited him.

"Find where they stayed," Hutchings told his men, who called at every hotel and lodginghouse, and finally among Plymouth's 250,000 inhabitants found a tiny furnished room over a shop, where a small man with a foreign accent, had stayed with another foreigner who had a large moustache.

"There was also another man in a gray car," said the shopkeeper. "I heard him tell Mr. Veltman 'not to come to the hotel.' "

Hutchings searched the room. On the hearth-shovel was dried cement. Behind the grate, a ball of tissue-paper.

Hutchings sent these to Plymouth analyst, Mr. Cyril Gill, who carefully straightened the paper and placed it under ultraviolet quartz lamps, then beneath refraction analyzers. "This paper recently wrapped a medicine-bottle," he said, "containing dentist's mouth-wash." The cement on the shovel matched exactly the cement in the gladstone bag.

Hutchings patiently found the hotel where the third man had stayed.

"I'm afraid that Mr. Korris, the gentleman you want, will not be back until the week end," said the manager. "He went off in his car, with friends."

"I saw him studying the A.A. map for the Stockport road," ventured the hall porter.

Hutchings had no photo, not much description, for Korris. But he had Hagendorf's photo. He circulated this to Stockport.

Within two days, Korris returned to Plymouth, firmly believing he had made no mistake that could have linked him with the sovereign swindlers. Hutchings took a bold chance, arrested him, sent Metropolitan C.I.D. officers to search his London home. There, in a purse behind a wardrobe, were nine Rand sovereigns!

Within a few days, came a message from Stockport police. "We have traced man answering Hagendorf's description to the Red Lion Hotel near here."

Hutchings interviewed this man.

"Ridiculous!" he stormed in flawless English. "My name is

Jack Carter—here are my papers, see! I was never in Plymouth in my life!"

Hutchings had observed Carter's fastidiously cleaned pearl-grey hat. He picked it up, folded back the inner sweat-band. There was a Plymouth cleaner's mark! Hagendorf, alias Jack Carter, went pale....

Veltman was picked up in London, trying to contact Korris.

At Plymouth Quarter Sessions in January 1937, Korris—the brain of the swindle—got five years. Hagendorf, three years (also four years at Leeds); and the pitiful little Veltman, eighteen months.

The dentist recovered only a part of his £2,300 . . . but Veltman's tooth is still on cotton wool in his surgery!

The Clue of the Cabbage Stalk

WHEN THE PHONE RINGS IN A POLICE
C.I.D. office, it might be murder . . . or somebody reporting
the theft of a handkerchief from her backyard wash-line.

The polished Squad cars nevertheless purr out, radios
crepitate, green bulbs glow on their dashboards. The detectives, bulky shoulders hunched under crumpled raincoats,
stand on doorsteps and ask their unwearying questions. The
hours go by. The hunt continues. . . . For there is no peace in
the soul of a good policeman until he has caught his criminal,
completed his report, ticked: "Inquiry closed" in the Headquarters Book.

So it was that in one of the large rooms along the carved
wooden galleries of Portsmouth City Police Headquarters,
lights burned until dawn for a fortnight.

Detective-Sergeant George N. Taylor, lengthy fingers
stained brown with chemicals, was pursuing a crime case. A

mug of tea on his laboratory bench had long since staled and curdled. He sipped it absently. It left a mahogany tide-mark across his lip. Sandwiches, stiff as cardboard, curled their edges beside him. He did not notice. He was busy with his instruments, among the tall cabinets stacked with fingerprint data—the microscopes, cameras, elaborate forensic apparatus.

Sergeant Taylor was in full, scientific pursuit of a thief who had stolen half a sackful of cabbages from the kitchens of the Golden Castle Hotel at Portsmouth. To convict him, he worked ninety hours, almost nonstop. He invented a new kind of police laboratory apparatus, made legal history, produced a contribution to the police textbooks of the world, that will be referred to long after he has finished his final day's duty.

The value of the stolen goods was 5s. 4½d. The value of Sergeant Taylor's job of work was no more—and no less—than if the theft had been that of the Crown Jewels.

The case began when the manager of the Golden Castle Hotel, whom we will call Mr. Arthur Levett, arose at six a.m., splashed his plainfully sleep-scorched red eyes with cold water and shivered into his clothes.

There had been little sleep for him that night. Mr. Levett had for weeks been alarmed at the way his kitchen vegetables were apparently disappearing. It was like a nightmare. He kept buying more, and more . . . yet never seemed to have enough.

Then, long after midnight, as he prowled the empty kitchens among the dying fires, Mr. Levett saw a half-sack of cabbages in the corridor outside the kitchen door. There was only the night staff on duty. They had no right in the kitchen. So Mr. Levett set his alarm for six a.m., determined to be awake before the first of his kitchen staff arrived, and see exactly what happened to those significant cabbages.

Just after seven a.m. a boy came whistling along the path. Gravel crunched under his careless feet. He had a bicycle. He slung the half-sack of cabbages into his bike carrier-basket, and was about to pedal away when Mr. Levett, his voice trembling indignantly, shouted: "Stop—thief!"

The lad gaped, eyes wide with innocent wonder. "Whatsa-matter, guv'nor?" he said.

When Mr. Levett had explained, the boy grinned cheer-fully. "That's all right, sir—I'm the son of your chef, you know —my father's name is Mr. Fransetti—he bought these cabbages yesterday, for our shop. They were delivered here for me to pick up this morning. We buy from the same wholesalers as you do, sir, an' it's easier for them to drop the stuff here."

Mr. Levett was not satisfied. He stormed around to the home of his chef, Mr. Fransetti—was rather dumbfounded to find that he actually was the proprietor of a greengrocery shop!

"That is to say, my wife—she keeps the shop," explained Fransetti with a gleam of unabashed white teeth. "And these are not your cabbages, Meestair Levett—see, I have here the receipts!

He produced a receipt, dated the previous day, from a Portsmouth vegetable wholesaler, for one half-sack of cab-bages. It was, indeed, one of the firms from whom Mr. Levett himself made his bulk purchases.

"Oh—er, well—of course . . ." Mr. Levett backed away towards the shop door.

"Not-a so queek!" shrilled Mr. Fransetti. "You have say I am a thief! I shall take this to the House of Lords! It makes to defame my character! You shall pay me plenty—you see!"

When Detective-Sergeant Taylor came on duty shortly before nine a.m., he found Mr. Levett palely seeking interview with him.

"This will ruin me, officer! What can I do?"

Taylor lit his pipe and regarded him benignly. "Do you get all your vegetables from this wholesaler?"

"Well, no—I get some from him and some from a farm at Hillhead, in Surrey."

"And which were these?"

Poor Mr. Levett shrugged, dejectedly. "How should I

know? One cabbage is just like another cabbage. How would anybody tell one from another?"

"That's something we shall have to discover," said Taylor. He commandeered a C.I.D. car, drove hurriedly to Fransetti's greengrocery shop. He was just in time to seize the half-filled sack of cabbages before they were emptied into the shop-bins. Then he turned his car's shining snout towards Hillhead, Surrey.

"Bless me," said the farmer, "how should I know which cabbages I sent to Mr. Levett? No, I don't sell any to that wholesaler where you say this Fransetti chap buys his stuff." He indicated a half-acre field, dotted with a myriad cabbage stumps. "Somewhere out of that field, they came."

Taylor examined the field. Some of the cabbage-stalks were yellow, withered. Others were fresh. He picked two sackfuls of the fresher stalks and roots, about 200 of them, and returned to his laboratory. There, he fitted up a prism and mirror, and two viewing lenses, side by side.

He put one of the stalks of the allegedly stolen heads of cabbage under one lens. Beneath the other, he placed the stalk of the root. The prism and mirror turned one image inside out, so that if the two stalks had been a stick of Blackpool rock split down the middle, the lettering on each would have been in readable sequence. Then he magnified them ten times— enough to make a bottle of beer as tall as a room.

Under his dazzlingly powerful microlenses, each green cabbage stalk, showing its inner circle of tiny white fringes, looked like the yawning jaws of a whale, with the fringes as the whale's crowded teeth. He began, painstakingly, to match them.

If you can imagine that you have 200 photos of badly blurred faces, each with mouth wide open as a dentist would see him; and that six of these 200 photos are in duplicate. Then, if you try to match the six duplicates with the correct half-dozen among the 200, you will have a very simplified version of what Detective-Sergeant Taylor had set himself to accomplish.

His cabbage stalks were no longer across than a penny. The points upon which he was attempting to match them, were the inner vegetation fringes, none bigger than a grain of sand, and numbering more than a hundred to the inch.

The job took him ninety hours, including the photographing of the magnified stalks. When he put the stalks under powerful arc lamps, they began to wilt and wither so quickly that he lost two specimens before he found a way of solving this new problem.

But when Mr. Fransetti appeared, loudly indignant, in Portsmouth City Police Court, there were four inescapable photographs, matched with the twin stalks, showing that the cabbages taken from his shop were grown on the field from which the Golden Castle Hotel was supplied!

It was his first offense. He was fined £10. "No hard feelings, I hope," he said, when he had paid his fine.

Detective-Sergeant Taylor blinked through swollen eyes. "Of course—no hard feelings," he said quietly. "It's all in the day's work."

He went back to the office. There were other matters piling up on his desk.

A Policeman's Job to Suspect Murder

HOW GOOD A POLICEMAN WOULD YOU be? Here was a file that called "murder" to the policeman upon whose desk it came, in the morning's mail. What would it have said to you? The story was like this:

Since late evening at Saxton Grange the stabled horses had been restless, sensing the dead man who sat slumped and stiffening in the garage next door.

He was their master, a burly young landowner now dead in the front seat of his green Chrysler, engine switched off. His solitaire diamond, big as an aspirin tablet, shone coldly upon his motionless finger and reflected without a wink the watery night moon.

There had been for some minutes such a strong stench of petrol fumes—raw and overpowering—in the garage that the cat had transplanted her September litter of blind kittens out into the loose-boxes where Fred Morton's big bay hunter and his wife's sixteen-hand blood roan stamped and fretted.

Suddenly the diamond on Fred Morton's dead finger sparkled with an orange glare—the car and garage had exploded into flames that burst through the roof and reached red tongues of fire out to the sky. The horses went mad.

The head groom, William Cairns, slept away in the village, and it was the under-groom, Ernest Brown, who came scampering from the low-roofed and spacious Grange House to rip apart the stable-doors. The horses thundered out, eyes white and wild.

"Mrs. Morton!" he shouted to the still silent windows of the Grange. "The whole place is on fire!"

The telephone had gone dead. Both cars were in the garage, burning like resin-torches. Brown trundled the unwieldy motor horse-box from the barn which was also now ablaze, and chugged off to get help from the farm bailiff, Mr. Murray Stuart.

At five-thirty a.m.—two full hours after the fire was first seen, the fire brigade arrived, breathless, engine spluttering, in time to save most of the farm buildings and the ancient Grange House itself.

The garage was destroyed, roof collapsed, both cars already cooling from stove-red heat into flaky, blistered grayness.

Mrs. Dorothy Morton had fled into the road with her personal maid Ann Houseman and two-year-old baby. She came back now, stood youthful, palely silent as the farm bailiff probed into the burnt green Chrysler with a hedge stake.

"D'you know what I think this is?" he said with countryman's bluntness. His stick had found a charred lump not much bigger than a loaf of bread. "It's all there is left of poor Freddy Morton."

The news was broken more gently to Mrs. Morton, who was led weeping into the house. Farmer Tom Hall wiped sooty sweat from his forehead. "This should be a lesson to us all not to touch drink again!"

The groom, Brown, echoed piously: "By God, you're right!"

They knew Freddy Morton had been fond of a few drinks. He had inherited money, but not content with the placid life of a country gentleman, had begun a prosperous business of his own—Cattle Factors Limited—with headquarters at Saxton Grange, buying farm beasts for cash and selling them on instalment to farmers throughout England.

Freddy Morton was barely twenty-eight years old, spoke Yorkshire dialect, despite his education, for friendliness' sake among the farmers. He drove hard bargains, drank hard, rode hard to hounds, was welcomed and respected by countrymen twice his years.

That evening after Morton's death, Brown the groom remarked morosely in the Sun Inn: "I was always afraid the boss would meet his death through drink in that car!"

The local policeman of the West Riding Constabulary came to the burnt-out ruins of the garage, poked around and made his report. His eyes were red sore. Constable Broadhead had been one of the first men on the job when the fire blazed up, had tried with vain valor to get in the blazing garage when it was suggested Freddy Morton might still be in one of the cars.

Now, seeking identification, Constable Broadhead picked out some melted coins, a few keys belonging to Morton. From the charred debris that lay thickly, still warm, under the twisted wreckage of the vehicles, he sifted and found a two-carat diamond. The gold ring had melted into hard yellow sludge.

To his superior, Chief Superintendent Wilfred Blacker at Wakefield H.Q., came the report of the village constable that there was no doubt it had been Frederick Morton, young squire of Saxton Grange, who died in the garage fire.

Cheerful Freddy Morton was a heavy smoker, particularly

after a few drinks. The night of his death he had called in at the Old George Hotel and later at the Boot and Shoe Inn at Peckfield, drank with the landlord and did a deal in cattle food. He told the landlady he was driving straight home to tea. It was then nearly nine o'clock at night.

The groom, Ernest Brown, said he was outside the barn when Morton finally reached the Grange, half an hour before midnight.

"The boss was 'clever side out' [drunk]," explained Brown. "He said he'd come for some petrol and was going straight out again. He did, too. I went to bed. It must have been three-thirty a.m. when I heard the horses and saw the fire."

Mrs. Morton and her maid had been in the kitchen, simmering jam, until midnight. They heard Morton's car come down the steep drive at eleven-thirty p.m., had not heard him go out again, but knew he did not enter the house.

An insurance assessor described both cars as completely ruined by fire. The petrol tanks had not exploded and the tank-caps were still on, but the drain taps were both opened.

To Chief Superintendent Wilfred Blacker came all this evidence, close-typed in a fat file upon his desk. To a less careful man it might have seemed nothing at all.

Nor had he much time to deal with it. For in the West Riding Constabulary district exist three million people upon nearly two million acres. It is England's most scattered police area, and across it the patrol-car radios stutter with far, gnat-thin voices. The beat is mostly country lanes and villages, and on to Chief Superintendent Blacker's desk spilled daily the skim of 4,000 rural constables' hourly jottings, of which the garage tragedy at Saxton Grange was just another. . . .

But work did not make Blacker too busy to miss the red glint of murder, when it sparkled out from his day's documents in the large gray-stone police headquarters at Wakefield. He perused the Morton file again.

Chief Superintendent Blacker leisurely ordered his car. He seldom rushed, never in his life looked like a policeman. He was large, pink-cheeked, very much a country squire with white moustache and with the manner of being chairman of some country cricket club. His eyes were mildly blue, his way deceptively courteous. When he drove to where the neat red chimneys of Saxton Grange stand behind their quiet hedgerows, he seemed merely a gentleman of the county paying a sympathy call upon the bereaved squiredom.

He spoke to Brown, the alert, thirty-three-year-old groom. "Bad business, Brown, this!"

"Aye, sir."

"They tell me you were in the yard when Mr. Morton came in."

"Yes."

"You saw him go out again?"

Brown nodded. He never wasted words. He was in appearance remarkably like many popular film stars with clever, sensual mouth, quick dark eyes, smart in brown suit, neat shirt, tie, well-cut breeches. A ladies' man, the Superintendent privately deduced.

"He was drunk?"

"He was, sir."

Then Blacker talked to the maid, Ann Houseman, was impressed by her air of integrity and bright intelligence.

"When did the telephone go out of order?"

She wrinkled her young forehead thoughtfully. "A call for Mr. Morton came about nine-forty-five p.m., important, from Scotland. The man said he would certainly ring again in fifteen minutes. But we never got it, so perhaps the phone broke between nine-forty-five and ten p.m."

"And you heard Mr. Morton come in at eleven-thirty, but didn't hear him go out?"

"I heard car wheels on the drive, coming down to the garage at eleven-thirty, sir. So did Mrs. Morton. We were both in the kitchen."

"He'd have to use a noisy third gear to get back up that steep drive, wouldn't he?"

"I expect so, sir."

"Where was Brown when the phone rang?"

"In the kitchen with us, sir. Then he went outside."

"Why?"

"I don't know, sir. He took a knife from the kitchen drawer." She showed him the knife. Blacker took it.

He went to the wrecked garage, studied the two twisted hulks, with the insurance assessor's detailed report in his hand, stooped to inspect the drain-tap on the Chrysler, then said to Constable Broadhead: "This tap needs a spanner, did you find one?"

"We did, sir—in the debris—it was an adjustable spanner— a nice one."

"Where is it?"

"Well, sir, Brown the groom claimed it—said it was his."

Blacker had a look at the horse-boxes, then spoke to the chief groom. "Why are the corn bins padlocked?"

Cairns hesitated.

"Well, sir, somebody was feeding extra corn to Mr. Morton's hunter, without my knowledge."

"Making the horse dangerous?"

"That's right, sir. I think it was Brown, trying to get me fired. He'd been head groom here before me, then had a quarrel with Mr. Morton and left. But he came back after three days. Mrs. Morton pleaded for him to be given a job, sir—and they gave him one under me. But he never liked it."

Superintendent Blacker went back to his office. "Send the remnants of that fire-destroyed body to the county pathologist. Ask the G.P.O. engineers to search the Saxton Grange telephone wires for where they've been deliberately cut with a knife, then send the cut ends of wire and this kitchen knife to Professor Tryhorn at Hull University and see what he can tell us—I believe he has some theories about metal striations.

"Also, ask the landlord of the Boot and Shoe Inn at Packfield if Morton was drunk or sober when he left him at nine-forty-five p.m."

The answer soon came from the landlord of the Boot and Shoe. "Mr. Morton was cold sober. He only had one beer, for we were talking business and he drove a very hard, cool bargain. Then he said he was going straight home—a ten minutes' drive."

The county pathologist, Dr. Sutherland, was soon on the phone. "Superintendent Blacker? This badly burnt portion of flesh is far too damaged for any scientific analysis, you know."

"Have a look anyway, Doctor," said Blacker. And that same afternoon came the answer. "Blacker? I say—there are two shotgun pellets in the pericardium!"

The G.P.O. engineers reported: "Yes, the Saxton Grange phone wires were deliberately cut, outside, by the wall."

And the famous Hull scientist said carefully: "I have matched the natural serrations of the knife-edge under high magnification with the striation-scratches on the cut phone wires. They are the same."

"Nobody has ever given evidence like that in a court of law before, Professor," said Superintendent Blacker. "Are you sure?"

"Most certainly!" boomed Professor Tryhorn. "It is a scientific fact! That knife cut those wires!"

There was one thing missing. Blacker went to Mrs. Dorothy Morton, to find it. "I'm sorry," he said with gentle politeness, "but I think Brown murdered your husband, and I also think you can tell me why."

Mrs. Morton went pale. She reached for a cigarette, and paced the room for a long time, smoking unceasingly. Stub after crumpled, red-stained stub was tossed agitatedly into the fire. Chief Superintendent Blacker waited.

At last she spoke. "Brown was in love with me," she said. "He thought I loved him, but I didn't. He was jealous of my husband."

"Did he think that if your husband died, you might marry him?"

"Yes, I think he did."

In his report to the Chief Constable of West Riding County, Chief Superintendent Blacker explained: "I have arrested Ernest Brown, for murdering Morton. He left the radio on loudly in the kitchen when he knew Morton was due home, so the women did not hear the car. He shot Morton in the garage, put the body in the car. Then at eleven-thirty he drove the other car into the garage—this was heard by Mrs. Morton and her maid, who supposed it was Morton returning home.

"At three-thirty a.m., when he knew there would be the longest delay in getting assistance, Brown set fire to the garage, having soaked his victim in petrol from the tanks of both cars. He hoped that traces of the shotgun wound would be destroyed, and he almost succeeded."

Almost . . . but not quite. Ernest Brown was found guilty of murder, and hanged.

When friends asked Chief Superintendent Blacker, after the trial, what made him suspect murder, he replied affably: "It's a policeman's job to suspect murder!"

THERE WAS A STRANGE CASE OF MURDER involving compulsion—the fetish murder committed in Newcastle, upon the body of Margaret Rice.

Young William Collins woke at two a.m. to wonder if the pretty girl he had attacked at midnight might still be alive. After he had smashed her skull and left her sprawled in the warm June grass . . . was she really dead, after all? Had it been only a trick of moonlight that made her wracked eyes seem to follow him?

Slowly, reluctant to leave his comfortable bed, Collins put on his trousers. He knew he had to make sure. He crept from his mother's house, up the next alley, across the wide highway of Claremont Road, to where the roving acres of Newcastle Town Moor stretched gray and quiet under the thin moon. He turned the girl's face and could see she was dead. He wiped his hands, returned satisfied to bed and slept. He had left no clues.

Next day the milk was late. The milkman, perched high on his delivery cart, had glimpsed the girl's body concealed behind one of the big emergency waterpipes that, in wartime 1942, were laid down Claremont Road ready to repair blitz damage. The milkman saw her limbs white upon the green dawn grass.

Newcastle C.I.D. officers studied her delicate face, like a fairybook illustration. Dew diamonds were in her dark hair. Her hands were carefully tended—even her toenails were pedicured to perfection. But her eyelashes were spiked with blood, for her skull had been smashed as one cracks the round top of a boiled egg with a little silver spoon.

Mr. F. J. Crawley, then Chief Constable of Newcastle, had staying as his guest Professor Louis C. Nickolls of the Home Office Forensic Laboratory. Before his breakfast, Mr. Nickolls knelt in the sparkling grass to examine the body.

"Somebody has disturbed her," he said. "The head was moved, some two hours after death. See, the little trickles of dried blood—they couldn't run uphill!"

Her smart grey check suit had been torn away. Her underclothing, which appeared to have been removed and then hastily replaced, for grass particles were caught in the inner folds, was fresh-laundered W.A.A.F. issue. Her handkerchief bore laundrymark "LIELL."

Detective-Sergeant (now Detective-Superintendent) John Barrett took charge. He traced the handkerchief to an A.T.S. station at Willington Quay, three miles down the Tyne. But at the camp, the handkerchief was claimed by an A.T.S. officer who was alive and unharmed.

He checked every other Service Camp for miles. None acknowledged a missing girl. All the miles of Town Moor stretched out, awaiting scrutiny. "Search it," said Barrett.

Fourteen feet from the footpath, the searchers found two ragged scraps of black vulcanite. The gunsmith identified them: "From the butt-handle of a heavy-calibre, old-fashioned revolver, probably a Webley .45."

By this time the mortuary photos had come through, showed

the skull cracked sharply, as might be by the lanyard ring of a heavy revolver.

Barrett published the girl's description in the local newspapers. By afternoon she was identified as Corporal Margaret Rice, W.A.A.F., stationed at Kenton R.A.F. Headquarters. Barrett demanded a woman officer should report to police C.I.D. office.

"Why did you say that Margaret Rice was not missing?"

The W.A.A.F. officer dabbed her eyes. "We all loved little Margaret—she was married a few weeks ago—we knew she was seeing her husband off on embarkation leave—we didn't want to report her as an absentee—we never thought of murder. . . ."

Nine hours of precious murder-hunting time thus lost! Barrett grunted, returned to his quest.

He traced Margaret Rice to the Newcastle railway station. She and her husband, an Artillery Lieutenant, had departed from billets for the station in a taxi. Nobody had seen them at the train.

Lieutenant Rice was recalled from Embarkation Camp, back to Newcastle. Anguish and fury were disciplined behind his tight-drawn young face. Margaret had been only twenty-three. He was not much older.

"I wanted her to take a taxi home," he said. "But she told me she wasn't scared of the black-out. No man would interfere with a girl unless he was encouraged, she said."

Then two girls were found, who had seen Margaret sipping coffee in the railway station refreshment bar after the train had left with her husband in it. So he was absolved.

Inspector J. M. Venner had been put in charge of a wide search of the murder zone.

"Pull up all the sewer-grids down Claremont Road," he ordered. "Examine down there, too."

The foreman of the Cleansing Department, Mr. P. Croucher, discovered a lady's watch. It had caught on the metal sheet grille that is placed in sewers for just such a purpose. The watch had stopped at two a.m. This was about two hours, as far as doctors could judge, after the girl had died.

Further along the road, down other grids, were a maroon glove, a silver bangle, a powder compact, pocket diary and haircomb. Young Rice steadfastly identified all these as his wife's. Then he turned his head away.

"Why rob a dead girl of such pathetic trinkets, then drop them down the drains?" asked Superintendent Weir. "Could it have been because the killer wanted to lay a false trail, set us seeking for a robbery motive?"

Detective-Sergeant Barrett had a psychological theory. "The murderer was a fetishist—he took the trinkets for the perverted pleasure of possessing them as souvenirs of what he had done to the girl. He kept them two hours. Then he came back and disturbed the girl again to see if she was properly dead. He dropped the trinkets down the sewers because he did not know there were baffle-plates to stop them disappearing for ever. He didn't dare keep them."

All of which added up to one vital clue to Newcastle police: "The murderer must live somewhere near where the girl was killed!"

Detectives began a careful inquiry among the residents of respectable Claremont Road district. They interviewed hundreds of people, took thousands of pages of statements.

Among all this mass of fact, lay two grains of value. The sharp eyes of Barrett did not miss them. 1. A young servant-girl, moon-gazing at her attic window on the murder night, had seen a man in some kind of blue uniform running down Claremont Road. 2. A dustman, Mr. William Kirkland, who was enjoying a drink in the North Terrace Tavern the day following the murder, reported to the police:

"We were talking about the murder. A young Merchant Navy chap joined in, put his hands around his own neck, and said 'I wonder if you can leave fingerprints on a girl's throat?' There was something about the way he said it that chilled me."

Police officers discovered there was a young Merchant Navy

man on sick leave with scabies, in Framlington Place, within fifty yards of the murder scene. It was just a routine inquiry. Detectives Checkley and Martin went to see him.

Handsome William Ambrose Collins, aged twenty-one, former pupil of the Royal Grammar School, received them readily, told all about his movements on the murder night, " . . . and my friend dropped me off in his car at the corner of Claremont Road just after midnight. I went straight home, and didn't see or hear anything.

"And what about that gun of yours?" asked Checkley casually.

Collins went pale. "How did you——" and that was enough. Checkley and Martin searched Collins's bedroom.

Under his pillow was a Webley .45 revolver. The vulcanite butt-plates were missing. Under his pillow also was an assorted collection of women's knickers. They had nothing to do with the murdered girl. But they seemed to link up with Barrett's theory of fetishism. All had been worn.

The two detectives searched the rest of the furniture. In a sea-chest in one corner, were the missing butt-plates. Each had a ragged piece chipped off. At Police Headquarters the two bits of vulcanite, found by Sergeant Barrett near the dead girl, were fitted into the gun-handles. Like a black, ominous jigsaw, they matched exactly!

Collins was taken out to the waiting police car, and driven from Framlington Place. The car wheels crunched the gravel in the gutter. Overhead in the June sunlight whispered the tall sycamore trees that had stirred all night over the body of his victim. . . .

Collins buried his head in his hands. There would be no clear skies over his own grave, he knew.

Looking back among some of my stories, I feel that I may have described the underworld and its denizens often as if they were a race of people apart from the rest of us. It is not true. A man may walk his respectable path—and suddenly a hole opens in the road, and he falls head over heels among the criminal underworld. Then, the way back becomes difficult.

I will tell you of a respectable man who became a convicted thief and got three years' imprisonment, which at once made him an "old lag" (a "lagging" is three years).

He was the mathematics master at a London day-school. His father was a dentist, who lived in an old-fashioned house along the Edgware Road, towards Lord's Cricket Ground. It had once been a very nice house, but the district deteriorated.

I will call him Ernest Green. He had a nice little wife, trusting and affectionate. When his father and mother died, and his two younger sisters went off—one to become a teacher, too, and the other to get married, Ernest and his wife found the house too big. They had no children.

It seemed a good idea to take lodgers. They took in a couple of bright, well-dressed young fellows who said they were car salesmen. They were gay, friendly, free with their money, and jolly company. After a little persuasion, Mr. and Mrs. Ernest Green finally went with them to the greyhounds, and to a drinking club. They had a wonderfully interesting evening.

The two gay sparks, Blackie and Lanky Johnny, admitted, when everybody was suitably mellow, that they were not car salesmen, but "professional backers." They made good money, they said, backing horses and dogs.

"We've got friends in the right places," confided Blackie, a bit drunk but not objectionable. "Want a coupla pair o' nylons, Mrs. G.?" Mrs. Green, who had never before taken more than one glass of sherry, giggled.

Next day, Blackie brought her half a dozen pairs of "export" nylons. "Little gift, from Johnny an' me," he said. But Ernest Green insisted upon paying for them. In his world, people did not accept gifts of such value quite so light-heartedly. They got him a couple of bottles of whisky. He paid for them. He mentioned to his colleagues at school that he could "get whisky or nylons, galore!" He was human, and couldn't resist showing off.

The history master was interested. "I suppose you couldn't get me a bottle of Scotch?" he said. "It's my father's eightieth birthday next week."

Ernest Green said he was sure he could. And—thanks to Blackie and Lanky Johnny—he did.

One day, Blacky and Lanky Johnny came home with a beautiful roll of export-only bird's-eye worsted cloth. It was splendid material—the sort of thing that just wasn't in the shops at that time.

"Fancy a few yards for a suit, chum?" asked Blackie airily. Ernest Green was delighted, and bought the cloth.

His new suit was admired by all his friends, who demanded

the name of his tailor. Before long, Ernest was selling suit-lengths to dozens of his friends. Practically every man at the local golf club, had a beautiful suit from Ernest; when the first roll was done, he got others.

Of course, it was inevitable what would happen. The Flying Squad got a search warrant and raided the respectable house of Mr. Ernest Green. They did it without a word of warning, without one preliminary inquiry. And they found five rolls of stolen cloth, three or four bottles of stolen whisky, etc., etc.

They did not find Blackie and Johnny. That wily pair had skipped. They were not picked up until months later, by which time a dazed and bewildered Ernest Green had been sentenced at the Old Bailey for receiving stolen goods. He got three years. Being a first offender doesn't count for much, when they get you red-handed for receiving.

I studied the dossier on Ernest Green's case. I became convinced that he was a fool—a great ass—but not a rogue. Yet here he was, convicted to three years. And a man who gets three years is not usually treated as a "star" prisoner (i.e. one likely to respond to special treatment). He gets put with the old lags.

I could guess what the old lags would do with Mr. Green. The underworld likes to meet a man with a bit of education, a respectable appearance or "flash front," who has proved himself gullible to crime. The underworld can find plenty of uses for him—to its own advantage.

I called to see his wife. She sat staring straight in front of her. She was proud, pale, and I could see that she was terribly hurt.

"I suppose," she said bitterly, "there will always be policemen poking their noses in at the door, for the rest of our lives, now?"

Poor little Mrs. Green needed just that little nudge, to upset her own balance, and turn her against society.

I said: "Why not go and get a job until this business is over? The police will not embarrass you, Mrs. Green."

She began to cry. "I'm going to have a baby," she said.

Troubles are like that. They come all of a heap. Installments were owing on the furniture. The life insurance policy was overdue. She had no money. It had all gone in legal fees, trying vainly to defend her husband in court.

The Discharged Prisoners' Aid Society said they would help with the furniture and life insurance arrears, and keep the payments going. Their lawyers helped Mrs. Green to sell the old house, and find a smaller one in a new district. She had her baby, and times were tough for her. I must admit that sometimes when my colleagues and I had backed a winner, we seemed to find it necessary to go and "make a few inquiries" in the district of Mrs. Green and her baby son. And sometimes when we hadn't backed a winner, we went, too. She was difficult and proud. But she had a baby to care for. She took the money, and wept about it.

At eight a.m. on a cold day, just over two years after he had been sentenced, the big, repulsive gates of Wormwood Scrubs opened, and Ernest Green stepped out. He'd earned all his good conduct remission. He was a "ticket of leave man," a convict on license.

He'd put on weight in prison. It's strange how men do. His old suit wouldn't fit him, and the Discharged Prisoners' Aid Society fitted him up with a new, tailor-made one, "in accordance with his previous station in life," as they put it. It was a good suit, although the cloth, naturally, wasn't export bird's-eye.

The old days, when a man left jail wearing a brown herringbone, or a grey herringbone, that every policeman could spot a street away, have now gone, I am glad to say.

He didn't, as some people think, have to carry his "ticket of leave." Nor was he ordered to stay out of public-houses and cinemas, and not go to the races. He didn't even have to report to the police. (This is only done when a man breaks his parole with the Central After-Care Association.) Before he left prison, Green had been given a copy of the rules, and a stamped envelope. He had to report in writing once a month to the Central After-Care Association. That was all.

He was a bit plumper, a bit paler, and quieter. He'd gone through a bad couple of years. Despite what some fools say, life is not fun in prison. Old lags can make a tolerable existence of it. But it is hell for a chap like Ernest Green.

The Discharged Prisoners' Aid people gave him £3, and the local Labor Exchange gave him as much help as they could. But who wants a schoolmaster, when he's done three years' prison? Certainly his former employers didn't.

I saw him a couple of nights after his release. He was at the dog-track. He was drunk. He was in bad company. It was understandable, though unfortunate. After a man has spent two years in prison, even two drinks will make him drunk. And an ex-convict has few friends—except ex-convicts.

I said: "Hullo, Ernest—backed any winners?" He scowled: "It's no blasted business of yours, is it?" I said: "No, I just came over to congratulate you on that fine baby son of yours, Ernest. He's a grand little chap." And when I saw Ernest's face change, as I had hoped it would, I added: "Can I come and talk to you tomorrow? I think there's an honest job you might be interested in."

He nodded. "O.K. Mr. Fabian—and thanks."

Next day, he came to see me. And I told him about the job we'd sorted out for him. A few decent bookmakers—and most of them are decent—had got together what is called "a set of bookmaker's tools" for Ernest. They found him a satchel, a blackboard, a stand, some printed tickets, a big colored umbrella.

"The boys heard you were a mathematics master, Ernest," I told him, "and they decided you must be good at arithmetic. So if you go to Lewes Races tomorrow and ask for Harry McTigue or Big Fred Smith or Walthamstow Billy, they'll fix you up with a clerk who knows the game, and see that you get a decent stand, and if you have a bad week, they'll see to that, too."

Ernest Green's sensitive, pale face twitched. I thought he was going to cry. But after a moment he laughed, and so did I.

Today, Ernest Green, as we called him, is a well-established turf commission agent, thoroughly respectable, and making quite a decent livelihood. Nobody on the race-tracks cares if he was in prison or not. All they—and the police—care about, is that he shall not go back again. And he won't, believe me, he won't.

To the Carlino gang, stealing cars looked an easy way to get rich.

Carlino had managed to seduce a Grade 1 clerk in the Petroleum Office. When owners of various makes of cars sent in petrol applications, this clerk schemed to mislay, here and there, a log-book. The Carlinos paid him £20 each for such dishonest strays.

Confident men with bunches of assorted car keys went out into the south of England, chose cars to match as nearly as possible the description in the log-books, calmly stole them. They fixed false number-plates, suitably bleached and overprinted the log-book entry . . . sold the cars openly at market price.

The Carlinos were making perhaps £500 a week, until Detective-Constable Charles Viveash, alert young fledgling of Reading Borough C.I.D., thirty miles from the busy sin of

London, took a slow stroll through the half-empty car park of
the Terminus Café.

He picked his way through the vehicles, scanned the Road
Fund License stuck to each windshield. It was the end of the
quarter. There just *might* be somebody overdue. The fact
that there did not seem to be much crime in Reading did not
discourage Detective-Constable Viveash from seeking it with
unquenchable zeal.

One car he examined was a blue Morris Twelve. The wind-
screen license showed tax £10, paid up to the year end, 1947.
Anything wrong with that? There was—but not one in a thousand men would have noticed. Constable Viveash happened
to be that one in a thousand. And from that moment the days
of the Carlino Gang were numbered.

What Viveash had noticed was that £10 was the tax for an
8-horsepower car, and this was a Twelve! He jotted down the
number and reported to his superiors.

"All right, Viveash," said the Chief Constable, who believed
in encouraging initiative among his men. "Go ahead and see
what you can find."

Viveash went to the local vehicle registration office. The car
listed under that registration number was not a blue Morris
Twelve at all. It was a black Austin Eight! So there *was* crime
in these quiet outskirts of the big city! Viveash turned up the
official files on the black Austin Eight. This required consider-
able research. The car had been purchased by a Mr. Jason for
cash from an Army scrap dump for £10, registered under
civilian license on Form RB6. Mr. Jason's address as given,
proved to be non-existent.

Detective-Constable Viveash went back into the quiet
streets to seek again the blue Morris Twelve with its puzzling
Austin Eight ancestry. He rediscovered it at last, being driven
by a lady of flawless repute, who, bewildered and indignant,
explained she had paid good money for the car from a man
named Luke, whose name and address appeared on the log-

book as previous owner. Viveash went seeking Mr. Luke. This
address, too, did not exist.

Dr. Wilson Harrison, Director of the Home Office Forensic
Laboratory at Cardiff, examined the log-book, confirmed that
the Tax Office stamp was forged, the car registration number
skilfully altered. He could not decipher the original registration number.

But the man named Luke had left two betraying clues
behind him. Viveash extracted both from the lady tricked into
buying the stolen car.

One—his description! Secondly, he had mentioned in the
garrulous, over-anxious prattle typical of the trickster, that he
knew the Falcon Inn, at Banghurst, very well.

To the staff of this hotel, C.I.D. men asked: "Do you know
anybody in the motor business, perhaps using the name Luke,
answering this description?"

The staff remembered a boastful, quick-talking, easy-
money man who *did* use the name Luke and had stayed at the
hotel. His correct address was in the hotel register.

Detective-Sergeant Leonard Allen and Viveash arrested
Luke just before dawn the next day. Luke, sleepy, startled, his
life force at lowest three a.m. ebb, lied clumsily. He did not
want to admit he was a mere white-collar stooge to a gang of
car-stealers (which he was). "I bought that car in good faith,"
he said, "from a man named Joseph Jason." He gave Jason's
address.

Jason was another agent of the Carlinos. Probably Luke
hoped that Jason would be able to give a more glib explana-
tion. And, indeed, having given no false address and not
having his name on the forged log-book, Jason might well have
provided a dead end to the trail. But Reading police decided
not to talk to Jason at once. Instead, they watched him all
that day.

At the news of Luke's arrest, Jason went straight to the
house of one Nino Carlino. The police went there, too. On

Carlino's lawn was a car, covered by tarpaulin. It was a Hillman, with number-plate removed. The chassis and engine numbers showed it had been stolen the previous afternoon.

Carlino was tough. He brushed his dark hair out of his beady eyes, and scowled truculently. "Somebody must have left it there last night," he said. "I'm a busy man. It was dark when I got home. Why should I notice?"

Young Detective-Constable Viveash grinned a little tiredly. For nearly three days he and Sergeant Allen had neither stopped nor slept. They did not stop now. Carlino's big house was searched. Clues were found that linked Carlino with a garage and repair business in Reading. Here were discovered log-books that proved to be "missing" from the District Petroleum Office.

The Hillman that stood accusingly on Carlino's lawn, was scanned by police experts for fingerprints. Carlino's were not on it. But those of "Curly" O'Connor were. The police knew his record. He had moved some months ago from London to Reading. The Metropolitan Police had not been sorry to lose him.

The chain was not yet complete. Constable Viveash went to the Petroleum Office, began to check carefully upon the employees. There was an elderly Grade 1 clerk, wearing a handmade suit and expensive silk tie, who had recently been putting in a great deal of voluntary overtime, working in various departments. From each of these departments where he had toiled with such surprising fervor after hours, car log-books had been missed. . . .

The Assizes trial lasted seven days. There were seventy-five witnesses. Detective-Constable Viveash, who presented the case for Reading Police almost single-handed, was in the witness-box six hours.

" . . . a most dangerous organization," said Mr. Justice Wrottesley. "It is obvious from the evidence that the thieves had been working all over the South of England, stealing cars and by repainting them, altering their registration-numbers and documents, were able to sell them to innocent purchasers. An organization of this kind can expect no mercy."

Nor did they get it. Sentences on the Carlinos totalled thirty-three years!

WHEN MARY HAGAN GOT HOME FROM school, her father sent her to buy an evening newspaper, after tea. Mary was fifteen, a well-behaved girl.

She did not return. At midnight anxious neighbors, with torches obediently veiled to the November 1940, blackout, found her slender body in a Home Guard blockhouse.

It was an ugly little concrete fortress on a railway bridge at Seaforth, near her Merseyside home. Train soot had hung black skeins upon its walls. The entrance was ankle-deep in dark water. Mary Hagan lay inside. She had been strangled.

The seekers rubbed her wrists, held a mirror to her lips to see if she could fog it with a stir of breath. It was the distressing instinct of simple-hearted folk unused to crime. But, in doing it, they trampled among possible murder clues like peasants in a wine-vat.

When Chief Superintendent Gregson, then chief of Lancashire Constabulary C.I.D., came hurriedly to the blockhouse, it had been cleared and roped off by Constable Dixon.

But there were signs of a multitude of blundering muddy feet. Gregson permitted himself a brief grunt of exasperation. He was a disciplined man.

The girl's body lay on dry earth inside the hut. Alongside her was an evening newspaper, quite fresh and folded. A wet boot-heel mark showed clearly upon it.

Rubbish littered and surrounded the blockhouse. Crumpled bits of paper and rag had been blown in by the wind. Dead leaves made a brown broth of the rain-puddles. Tins, cigarette-packets, matches, had been tossed through the gun-slits.

Police with stirrup-pumps sucked the quagmire from the concrete floor, filtered it, laid articles on blotting-paper at C.I.D. Headquarters. Detectives fingered them carefully.

There were many false clues. An example: a dirty handkerchief, marked "G. Rimmer."

In West Lancashire there are a large number of Rimmers. All were visited. Detectives went to every Army camp, searched nominal rolls for Rimmers. All the ships in Liverpool harbor were boarded. All were useless. The handkerchief had nothing to do with the murder.

Meanwhile detectives were busy taking boot- and shoe-heel prints from every person among the search-party that had found Mary Hagan's body, from every person traced as having crossed the railway bridge near the blockhouse that murder night.

Even Mary Hagan's father, who had led the search, matched his shoe-heels with the others. None was identical with the heel-mark on the newspaper.

The Home Guard were paraded and cross-examined. No clues.

All this . . . in a few days . . . with every man of the C.I.D. toiling sleeplessly, sipping flask coffee, eating sandwiches from raincoat pockets.

Traces of milk-chocolate were found in Mary Hagan's

teeth. Among a fold of her clothes had been a bit of wrapping-paper from a chocolate-bar.

Further in the blockhouse debris, under the shadow of a darker corner, was more silver paper from the same chocolate bar. It matched like a jig-saw.

A cotton thread was caught up in this crushed tinfoil. It bore traces of zinc ointment, was also impregnated with an antiseptic.

Under the puddle of black water upon which the tinfoil had precariously floated, was a dirty bandage, shaped to fit a thumb.

"It is a strip of gauze from an Army field dressing," reported Dr. J. B. Firth, of the Home Office Forensic Laboratory at Preston. "I can identify it by the antiseptic with which it is impregnated. Also zinc ointment has been used with this bandage—quite unnecessarily."

No military medical orderly would have put zinc ointment on a field dressing. Indeed, no soldier on duty would have opened his field-dressing packet to bandage a thumb injury.

Hospitals were visited, chemists, doctors. Nobody remembered a soldier, airman, sailor, Home Guard, coastguard, with an injured thumb.

Detectives were still busy in the streets around Brook Vale railway bridge, questioning people. "Did you go near the blockhouse that night? Did you see a man? Have you ever seen a man loitering near the blockhouse?"

For the lock had been deliberately broken several days before.

Finally . . . "Yes," said a young married woman, "a soldier tried to trip me up on the bridge near the blockhouse several days ago."

Next a schoolgirl: "There was a soldier on the bridge who looked at me and walked towards the blockhouse. I waited until some people came up before I dared cross the bridge."

Detectives went from door to door. "Have you seen a soldier around this district with a bandaged thumb?"

"Yes," said the barmaid in a local public-house. "He was a tall young man in the Irish Guards."

Records were searched for soldiers of the Irish Guards who had relatives in Seaforth district, and who had leave passes to Liverpool.

On November 15, 13 days after the murder of Mary Hagan, a 28-year-old Irish Guardsman (I will call him Michael Hogan, although that is not his name) sat in Seaforth Police Station.

On his thumb was a newly-healed scar.

Police searched his mother's house. They found a lump of damp gauze in the bathroom. It had been used as a child's face cloth.

It was an Army field dressing! A strip had been torn from it.

Under microscopes, the gauze from the bathroom and the thumb-bandage found on the murder scene were enlarged to the size of jacket-sleeves. Each had a double row of irregular stitching. They matched. So did every fibre of the gauze. It was almost like comparing fingerprints.

But Gregson was careful. He sent for hundreds of Army field dressings, had them opened at Manchester College of Technology and compared against the thumb bandage. . . .

Every one had different stitchings. None matched—except the one at Hogan's house!

"Now," Detective-Inspector Floyd told Hogan, "let's have a look at your boot-heels."

The left heel of Hogan's shoe matched exactly the mark on the newspaper found beside the dead girl.

Hogan's mouth twisted. His eyes filled with tears. "I'll tell you," he said shakily, "I—I don't know what made me do it . . ."

At Liverpool Assizes on Monday, February 17, 1941, he was found guilty of murder, and later hanged.

FOR THE SAKE OF HIS YOUNG WIFE, whom he adored, Jerry Hayward tried to be careful about murdering the landlady of the New Inn. He did not want any mistakes to destroy his own happiness.

Jerry Hayward had decided the landlady of the New Inn at Hayfield was worth murdering when he discovered she kept £50 in her bedroom.

He needed £50. He had lost his job as commercial traveler with a soap firm. His wife did not know he owed this firm £70. But she did know they owed rent on their white cottage that overlooked the wild, grand Derbyshire valley three miles from Glossop, with mountain Kinder Scout dignifying its skyline.

They owed hire-purchase money on the furniture. All Jerry Hayward got now was 25s. each Friday from New Mills labor exchange. Even this hurt his pride.

And half a mile down the valley, at the desolate New Inn, was a cashbox with £50, and only a woman to guard it.

For the New Inn did its big trade at evening, and the landlord, Arthur Collinson, went each morning to work sandpapering in Glossop. He left his wife Amy alone to attend sparse mid-day thirsts.

Jerry Hayward had discovered where she hid the cash-box. When he lingered over ale in the bar, he always listened to Mrs. Collinson's footsteps as she went up to the bedroom overhead for extra cash to refresh the till. Her feet travelled six paces into the far side of the room above . . . paused . . . clink of thin metal, obviously not a safe . . . six paces retraced to the bedroom doorway. Jerry had good ears.

He laid his plans. Knock her down when she was alone. Cut her throat. Make it seem suicide. Take only some of the cash. Disturb nothing. They would think she had killed herself because her accounts wouldn't balance.

At night, in the darkness, Jerry Hayward thought it out while his young wife slept unrealizing beside him.

Suppose he got splashed with blood when he cut her throat? Jerry Hayward smiled with secret exultation into the room's shadows. Easily fixed. His rubber mackintosh. Blood would wash straight off it. His white rubber collar, which his pride despised, could soon be wiped. Blood specks elsewhere? Jerry Hayward planned the perfect answer.

On Friday, November 11, 1927, he cut his cheek shaving, dabbed it repeatedly with the white bathroom towel. There was his alibi!

At about ten-fifteen a.m. the boilerhouse men at Clough Mills, some distance from the inn, would see him heading for the bus. They usually did. On November 11 he took care they saw him.

At ten-thirty exactly he struck Mrs. Amy Collinson's skull with a cudgel as she knelt cleaning her kitchen grate. She never knew what hit her.

At ten-forty-five, breathing sedately, Jerry Hayward climbed on to the fussy little country bus to New Mills to draw his weekly 25s. dole. In his mackintosh pocket was £40. Mrs. Collinson now lay dead. Her own kitchen knife shone metallically in the red gash across her throat. . . .

Prompt at 11 o'clock the bus halted to observe the two minutes' silence of Armistice Day. Jerry Hayward shut his eyes and thought his own strange thoughts as he waited while 120 seconds ticked away beside the bleak winter Derbyshire hedgerows, five miles up the lane from where he had just done murder.

At six p.m. that day the landlord of the New Inn chugged punctually home on his motor-bike. At his tavern door waited villager Amos Dawson.

"Can't get in, Arthur—haven't been able to get in all day. Y'missus has niver open t'door!"

Puzzled, Mr. Collinson entered his unlit inn. No fire, no fragrant simmer of tea. His wife lay stark dead against the flowered pattern of the far wall, among blood. Their grate stood gray and cold.

Assistant Chief-Constable James Garrow, of Derbyshire County Police, brought his murder-team by car from Derby.

"Not suicide," he said. "She couldn't cut her throat and leave the knife in the wound. Death convulsions in the fingers would drag the knife away."

So it was murder. "Anything stolen?" Mr. Collinson was asked. White-faced, he checked his cash-box. "About £40," he said at last.

The chief of Derbyshire's C.I.D., Chief Superintendent Walter Martyn Else, watched, intrigued. "You always keep the cash-box in that tin trunk in the bedroom? And is the room just as you found it—no drawers disturbed, cupboards opened? Then who else knew where you hide your cash-box?"

Mr. Collinson, his throat parched with a lump of dry grief that could not be swallowed, replied slowly: "I suppose most of the regular customers would be able to guess. They can hear us down in the bar as we move about the bedroom."

The murder team went to work on that. Superintendent McDonald, Inspectors Banham and Cordin, catalogued all the local drinkers, prepared details of where each man had been between ten a.m. and noon that fatal morning.

Two had been seen near the inn. One was that young fellow Jerry Hayward from the white cottage across the valley.

"I happen to know he's a bit hard up lately, sir," volunteered the local constable, P.C. Glynn, who "happened to know" everything about the folk of Hayfield, as is the valuable way of village policemen.

Meanwhile, in the white cottage across the valley, Jerry Hayward was enjoying the sight of his young wife's shining eyes as she tried on delightedly a pair of warm winter gloves he had brought for her, and placed two £1 notes in her threadbare purse.

"My sister met me in Manchester and gave me the gloves and money for you," he explained.

There was a knock upon the door. The police had called. But in face of inquiring Inspector Cordin Jerry Hayward smiled. "Yes, I did call at the inn for cigarettes—just before I caught the bus to New Mills. I wasn't there two minutes, Mrs. Collinson was all right then."

When police searched his clothes and found blood-specks on his tie, Jerry Hayward appeared untroubled. "Must have been my shaving cut." He showed them the blood-dappled towel.

The astute brain of Chief Superintendent Martyn Else absorbed this alibi instantly. "Then examine his hat," he instructed. "Shaving cuts do not drip above the neck. And there *must* have been blood, for the skull injuries indicate two blows."

Thus, in a remote Derbyshire village, Martyn Else introduced to police experts of the world his proven theory that blood spatters only when more than one blow is struck. The first blow merely brings blood welling up. It is the further blow that scatters it.

Upon the fawn trilby of Jerry Hayward under police laboratory microscopes were seen fifteen tiny blood-specks.

The white cottage was searched. Up a bedroom chimney was £32 5s. 11½d.

"Money I owe to my last employers," explained Hayward glibly. "They will tell you I never handed over £70 of accounts I collected last September before I lost my job."

Derbyshire police took the serial numbers of the £1 notes to the Inland Revenue in London. "One of these £1 notes was issued on October 24, 1927," a Treasury official reported.

Assistant Chief Constable Garrow noticed cobwebs disturbed on top of a disused cistern in the New Inn outhouse, and found a blood-stained cudgel made from lead piping wrapped in brown paper.

The plumbing in Hayward's house was searched, while his wife watched anxiously. From the kitchen waste-pipe a length had been sawn where it emerged from the outside wall.

The sawn edges of the cudgel and waste-pipe matched exactly. In Hayward's toolshed was a fine-tooth saw, its cutting edge still glittering with lead-dust.

In Hayward's jacket pocket, where he had carried the murder weapon to the inn, were similar grains of lead sawdust.

Three months afterwards, at Derby Assizes, he was found guilty. "I have nothing more to say," he commented. And his voice broke.

The voice of Mr. Justice Hawke, as he pronounced the court's inevitable edict, also faltered. For this had been his first death sentence, too.

MAXIE THE DWARF LEANED AT THE corner of drab Vernon Street picking his teeth with a six-inch nail.

His tattered jacket had belonged to a schoolboy. It hung nearly to Maxie's knees. His long, muscular arms bulged and protruded at each knee.

Suddenly he snapped the six-inch nail between his fingers, doubled it like a wire hair-pin.

'Gi'es a fag!" he grunted.

His doss-house mate, Davey, jumped. He was afraid of the dwarf.

"Eh, Maxie lad—I've no fags—see!" He turned out his musty pockets anxiously.

The dwarf watched. The mill chimneys of Nelson's grim Lancashire skyline loomed tall and gray behind him.

"Tha'art useless!" he snarled. "C'mon!" It was nearly lunch-time.

They halted at a phone box. Maxie sneaked two phone-books, hid them under his jacket, led the way into a public-house filled with mid-day drinkers.

He glared around the noisy bar. "I'll wager a couple of pints nobody here can tear these two phone-books with bare hands!"

The beer drinkers glanced down amusedly. "It's a bet, lad!" said a sturdy Lancashire farmer. He seized the two phone-books. His knuckles blanched. He tugged vainly, cheeks crimson.

"Nay," he panted at last. "A little chap like the'll niver do it if I cannot."

Maxie the Dwarf grinned, took the phone-books. His fingers dug into them like derrick-hooks. Steadily, contemptuously, he ripped them into halves.

The farmer paid for two large beers. "You'll be murdering somebody with those hands of yours, lad," he said good-humoredly. "They'll get you hanged, you see!"

Max wiped beer-froth on his tight coat-sleeve and grunted. . . .

At closing time the dwarf and his companion left. Max took a kick at a perky, white-and-tan fox terrier that had stopped to sniff amiably at him. An old woman snatched it up, glared and shuffled away. Her clothes were in rags.

"Nay, Shorty," laughed a bystander, "if you'd been nice to her dog she'd have given you a shilling. She's got a fortune hidden in her house."

The dwarf's eyes narrowed. "Who says?"

"I'm telling you the truth. She spends nothing on herself. Lives for her dog—a proper miser, she is."

Four days afterwards, on June 22, 1936, Detective Chief-Inspector Fenton of Lancashire Constabulary thrust through a group of neighbors outside the little house of old Ruth Clark-son, in Clayton Street.

"I'm glad you've come, Inspector," said a woman. "Something's wrong. She's not taken her dog for a walk for three days."

Fenton nodded, knocked authoritatively. There was no reply. The dingy curtains remained drawn. He pushed his burly shoulder against the door. The lock splintered.

Inside was a tangle of hoarded belongings. A narrow alleyway threaded among them. Old barrels, stuffed with worn shoes, discarded tins. Enamel mugs in which tea and cocoa had been brewed festooned the litter. From the living-room chandelier a bicycle lamp hung by string.

Under the table, among a heap of earthen pots, syrup-tins, rags, lay the body of old Ruth Clarkson, her skull ferociously crushed. Her torn garments had been ripped in a search for a moneybelt or valuables.

Upstairs, in the bedroom, Fenton found the old lady's dog. It was strangled, a blood-matted bruise on its ribs.

Beside the dead woman was a heavy tire lever, sharpened at one end to make a burglar's instrument. Blood and gray female hair stuck to it. Nearby was an overturned chair. The intruder must have climbed on to the chair to reach the cupboard door.

When police photographs had been taken, fingerprint experts had searched among the litter, and the body removed, Fenton came back to the room and regarded the overturned chair thoughtfully.

"Why did the thief need to stand on a chair to reach that cupboard?" thought Fenton. "He must have been a very little man!"

His gaze strayed to the mantelpiece, where the old newspapers were undisturbed over the vases. Elderly ladies frequently hide money in vases on the mantelpiece. Yet the thief had not ransacked these. Was it because they were too high?

Fenton sent his detectives to visit all the pawnshops, jewelers, second-hand shops for miles around.

"Have you been buying any bits of jewelry, silver, watches

or gold coins from a chap very much shorter than average height?" they asked.

And soon, on Fenton's desk, a strangely assorted hoard began to amass. A gold breast-watch, a silver mesh purse, a silver brooch, a gold ring, a thin gold chain with pendant.

"And the description is the same in each case, sir," said his assistant. "Sold within the last few days by a little chap about 4 ft. 6 in. tall, shabbily dressed.

"Find him," said Fenton.

That was not difficult. But when C.I.D. officers brought in the diminutive tramp known as Maxie the Dwarf, whose real name was Max Mayer Haslam, the little chap was indignant.

"Me? What have I done?" he inquired virtuously.

Chief-Inspector Fenton remembered the bruise on the dead dog's ribs. He sent Max Mayer Haslam's boots to Dr. Arnold Renshaw at the Manchester Pathology Laboratory.

"If there's a dog at the lodginghouse where Haslam has been staying, get samples of its blood and hair," he ordered.

There was a dog—a Pomeranian.

"I have discovered dog-hairs and blood between boot-sole and toe-cap," reported Dr. Renshaw. "The hairs are not those of a Pomeranian dog—they belonged to a wire-haired white-and-tan fox terrier."

Fenton searched the room that Haslam had shared with other men. He found nothing helpful. But the back-yard step of the lodging-house showed certain scratches. Chief-Inspector Fenton removed the entire step, took it to police headquarters. The scratches matched exactly with the sharpened edge of the tire-lever that had been the murder weapon. Maxie the Dwarf was found guilty at Manchester Assizes, November 1936, and hanged.